Social Welfare
or Social Control?

Social Welfare or Social Control?

SOME HISTORICAL REFLECTIONS ON

Regulating the Poor

EDITED BY

Walter I. Trattner

THE UNIVERSITY OF TENNESSEE PRESS

KNOXVILLE

Library of Congress Cataloging in Publication Data

Main entry under title:
Social welfare or social control?
  Bibliography: p.
  Includes index.
    1. Public welfare—United States. 2. Piven, Frances
Fox, Regulating the poor.
I. Trattner, Walter I.
HV95.S618 1983   361.6'0973   82-15901
ISBN 0-87049-374-4
ISBN 0-87049-375-2 (pbk.)

CONTENTS

Social Welfare
or Social Control?

INTRODUCTION

WALTER I. TRATTNER
University of Wisconsin-Milwaukee

This book is the product of a session on "Social Welfare or Social Control?" held at the April 1980 meeting of the Organization of American Historians.[1] That session stemmed in large part from my belief that the time had come for historians of social welfare to pay serious critical attention to the idea of social control in general and to react, in particular, to Frances F. Piven and Richard A. Cloward's *Regulating the Poor: The Functions of Public Welfare,* published some nine years earlier.[2]

Over the last two decades the historical literature on social welfare has come to be dominated by those who have asserted that native-born upper- and middle-class whites have used the nation's welfare institutions and organizations — public and private agencies, settlement houses, the criminal justice system (especially juvenile courts), the public schools, and the like — not to help the needy but to direct and to control their behavior.[3] In fact, so pervasive has this notion become that David Rothman, one of the authors of a recent and very articulate statement on the "limits of benevolence," has suggested that there now even exists a widespread and acute suspicion of the very idea of doing good: "Whereas once historians and policy analysts were prone to label some movements reform, thereby assuming their humanitarian aspects," Rothman has written, "they are presently far more comfortable with a designation of social control, thereby assuming their coercive quality. . . . The prevailing perspective looks first to how a measure may regulate the poor," not to how it might relieve or help them, he concluded.[4]

Ironically, as James Leiby indicates in his reflections on "Social Control and Historical Explanation" near the end of this book, the term *social control* originally had benign rather than sinister connotations. It was used to describe those processes in a society that supported a level of social cohesiveness sufficient for its survival, including measures that enabled the helpless and the needy to function within the social order. Accordingly, social control not only had to exist in order to provide coherence and consistency in society, but from a sociological perspective it was *the primary objective* of social welfare institutions and their personnel, especially those we now call social workers.[5] More recently, however, many writers have used the term *social control* to describe the way in which they believe members of the so-called ruling class, or specific elitist groups, manipulated and regulated the attitudes and behavior of members of the lower classes or other deprived groups, *in order to promote their own self-interest.*

Whatever the specific causes of this change in definition and usage of the term, there certainly were ample reasons for raising questions about the older premises of American social history and policy. Basically, however, the challenge to humanitarianism and moral considerations as masks for intrusion, domination, and self-interest was a reflection of the unsettled mood, especially the widespread cynicism and alienation, that characterized the 1960s and 1970s, a mood that, in turn, led to the emergence in the scholarly community of the so-called New Left.

While the New Left and its ethic certainly had roots in the past, especially among historians,[6] the impetus for this radical thrust came largely from the events of the last two decades. The prevailing history, which minimized social ills and conflict and celebrated mainstream America and the notion that the nation's citizens, all its citizens, had been treated fairly by an affluent, just, and peaceful society — "The Cult of the American Consensus," to use John Higham's words — became very difficult, indeed impossible, to accept by many younger scholars coming to maturity at a time when the seamier side of the nation and many of its actions was all too evident.[7] Among other things, there was the Bay of Pigs invasion launched by a new young President who, just a few months earlier in a stirring inaugural address, had pledged generous aid to underdeveloped nations, firm support for the United Nations, and a quest for world peace — followed by a shallow defense of the adventure by members of his administration, including such notable "liberals" as Adlai Stevenson and Arthur Schlesinger, Jr.

Then there was the civil rights movement, which forced all Americans to see the depths to which racism permeated virtually every aspect of American society and which encouraged not only black

Americans but also members of various other racial and ethnic groups, including Indians and Hispanic-Americans, to grow more self-conscious and boisterous; clearly, the fire under the alleged melting pot began to flicker, if not disappear, during these years.

The painfully incomplete realization of the "American dream" was further revealed by the publication in 1962 of Michael Harrington's *The Other America*. Then came a number of other books that further documented the existence of a severe and growing poverty problem, not only for members of various minority groups but also for older people, widows, divorcées, and others of all colors and backgrounds.⁹ Shortly thereafter came the riots that rocked hundreds of urban communities across the nation, obvious manifestations of widespread oppression, longstanding poverty, and great despair.

Of significance also was the women's liberation movement, which exposed the sexist nature of American society and widespread discrimination against women not only in education and in employment but in most other areas of American life as well. Similarly, the development of the "counterculture" and the emergence of the gay liberation movement brought into the open yet other forms of intolerance and prejudice — against those whose lifestyles or sexual preferences deviated from the majority. The student movement, a protest against the authoritarianism and the sense of indifference expressed by the nations's colleges and universities toward their students, further opened some eyes.

Meanwhile, the Vietnam War and the anti-war movement were having their disillusioning effect. Especially troublesome was the disparity between the professed idealism and morality of the state's "official" policy and the obvious sordidness and immorality of the affair, including support of the Saigon dictatorial elite and destruction of the Vietnamese peasants in the name of freedom. Furthermore, the frequent resort to violence at home, including the clubbing of peaceful demonstrators by the forces of "law and order," not only in the streets of Chicago during the 1968 Democratic National Convention but on countless other occasions as well, had a revealing effect. To many, the nation had an overblown federal bureaucracy, which was on the one hand remote from, and on the other hand often arbitrary and oppressive toward, the people it was supposed to serve. Compounding the problem was the so-called imperial presidency, the pathological result of which was a chief execu-

tive who believed, and even publicly argued in defense of the Water-
gate affair, that in the name of national security he could do essentially anything he pleased, even if it violated the law. No wonder
a group of younger scholars began to call into question—were almost compelled to call into question—the alleged benignity of the
American experience and to confront what to them seemingly was
the myth of a democratic, egalitarian, affluent, and peaceful America and the reality of an imperialist, exploitive, poverty-stricken,
strife-ridden, and authoritarian society.[9]

Not surprisingly, the nation's social welfare institutions and programs, even the concept of benevolence itself, came under intense
scrutiny and attack. Altruistic rationales were not very marketable
in an age of cynicism—especially in light of the overall failure of
the "war on poverty" and the persistence of so much hardship, poverty, destitution, and dependency. As popular groups and writers
stressed the glaring weaknesses they perceived in other areas of
American society, historians of social welfare challenged the ideal-
istic and moralistic interpretation of welfare programs and the reasons for their implementation. Humanitarian and reformist rhetoric aside, progressive ideas did not shape social policy, the critics
argued. Rather, the changes and "reforms" that occurred were designed by the upper classes to manipulate and co-opt those below
them; control of the poor by shaping their opinions and world view,
by buying them off with short- or long-term but inadequate benefits, and, when necessary, by using repressive force, has enabled the
elite to prevent the serious disruption of society, preserve the capitalist system, and maintain its social and economic advantage.

One of the clearest, most forcefully presented, and influential of
these works stressing social welfare as a means of social control was
Piven and Cloward's well-written and widely heralded *Regulating
the Poor*. Like many of the other more radical revisionists, Piven,
a political scientist, and Cloward, a sociologist and social worker,
have straddled the chasm between social theory and social activism,
between the classroom and the ghetto storefront; they not only have
been theorists and teachers of urban political dynamics and social
work, but for years they have been deeply involved in the social welfare community as well. Indeed, as some of the essays in this book
correctly indicate, both are battle-scarred veterans of the so-called
welfare rights movement[19] and many of the other frays about which
they so passionately wrote in this and their many other publica-

tions, including two later but closely related books — *The Politics of Turmoil* and *Poor People's Movements.*

The Politics of Turmoil: Essays on Poverty, Race, and the Urban Crisis was perhaps the clearest product of their involvement in various social welfare reform movements of the 1960s. For the most part, it was a collection of previously published articles which, taken together, both documented the existence of huge pools of poor individuals and families who were eligible for but were not receiving public assistance, and called upon activists to mobilize those people in an effort to ameliorate their condition, drive up the welfare rolls, and thereby reform the system.[11] In other words, it was not merely an analysis of poverty and conventional institutions that seemingly were designed to help the poor but that, they alleged, really operated to maintain an oppressive system; it also was a strategic and tactical manual for challenging that system through disruptive confrontation which, in their estimation, was the only leverage the poor had on those in power.[12]

Piven and Cloward's more recent work, *Poor People's Movements: Why They Succeed, How They Fail,* also dealt with the politics of the welfare state and was designed to further document their contention that the powerless can gain power, or at least challenge social inequities, only through mass insurgency. Through a study of four mass-action movements in recent American history — one by unorganized unemployed workers in the early 1930s and another by those who affiliated with the c.i.o. later in that decade, the civil rights struggles of the late 1950s and 1960s, and the welfare rights demonstrations of the 1960s and early 1970s — the authors attempted to demonstrate that once mass protest movements become structured they tend to become bureaucratic and self-restrained, and hence unsuccessful. Once again, the message was clear; the only way the poor will gain any meaningful social and economic reform is through extended protests and mass disruptions; if and when those efforts turn to organizations and electoral politics, they will fail.[13]

In *Regulating the Poor,* as in their two later works, Piven and Cloward mixed history, economics, political science, and sociology in an effort to explain the socio-political and economic origins and functions of America's social welfare system. Not surprisingly, they expounded in that work the same rather harsh theses that ran throughout their later books — that public welfare programs and institutions have not been, and are not, philanthropic or benevolent in nature; rather, they are intended to maintain social and political tranquility and to force the poor into the labor market. Assistance is given to the needy not out of concern for their plight—after all, Piven and Cloward argue, aid is given only when the poor are driven by privation to resort to violence—but rather out of concern for the stability of the social and economic orders and the self-interest of the elite who control them. Relief, in other words, was designed to be, and has succeeded in being, an effective means of manipulating the poor—keeping them under control and occupied in low-income, menial labor. To quote Piven and Cloward: "Relief arrangements are initiated or expanded during the occasional outbreaks of civil disorder produced by mass unemployment, and are then abolished or contracted when political stability is restored. Expansive relief policies are designed to mute civil disorder, and restrictive ones to reinforce work norms. In other words, relief policies are cyclical—liberal or restrictive depending on the problems of regulation in the larger society with which the government must contend."[14] Self-interest, not humanitarianism, as the traditional liberal account would have us believe, is the driving force behind public relief measures in this, the classic social control interpretation of social welfare.

While *Regulating the Poor* (and the so-called Piven and Cloward thesis) did not receive universal acclaim,[15] it was, on the whole, exceptionally well received. Indeed, the work immediately became, and remained, required reading for much of the scholarly community, especially college students and professors interested in urban poverty and public policy, and it also attracted widespread popular attention and approval.[16] Yet, much of the work has never undergone close critical analysis from historians. Indeed, as surprising as it may seem, as Andrew Achenbaum points out in his essay, the book was reviewed in only two major historical journals, and then only in passing fashion.[17] Furthermore, even those social scientists who have scrutinized the work have, for the most part, concentrated on the authors' treatment of the 1960s; with very few exceptions, they offered little sustained criticism or analysis of the earlier historical sections of the book. Clearly, the time has come for historians to pay serious attention to this important and widely acclaimed study.

This book, then, is a belated but badly needed attempt to provide, as the subtitle indicates, some historical reflections on Piven and Cloward's *Regulating the Poor*. More specifically, it is designed to test the central thesis of that work — to determine, in other words, whether public welfare programs (and the relief rolls) in America have expanded during times of disorder resulting from mass unemployment and, conversely, whether the relief system has contracted during times of stability and widespread employment, as Piven and Cloward have argued.

As the reader will discover, the authors of the first three essays, John Alexander, Raymond Mohl, and Muriel and Ralph Pumphrey, examine periods in American history Piven and Cloward chose to ignore — the Revolutionary and post-Revolutionary era, the late nineteenth century, and the first three decades of the twentieth — and all express serious doubts about Piven and Cloward's claims. So, too, does Andrew Achenbaum, the author of the fourth essay, who surveys territory Piven and Cloward did traverse in their book — the 1930s, the Social Security Act, and treatment of the aged — and simply concludes that they were wrong. Their data, in other words, is not only scanty and highly selective, according to these critics, but their interpretation of it is incorrect as well.[18] James Leiby, the author of the fifth contribution, an expanded version of his informal comments at the O.A.H. meeting, has yet other criticisms of Piven and Cloward and their work (as well as that of the other essayists).

Piven and Cloward, in turn, in a spirited response accuse their critics of writing flawed, even shoddy history — of engaging in overblown rhetoric, of confusing ideas with practice, of using faulty statistical methods, of misinterpreting their work and deliberately overstating their arguments in order to better refute them, or at least attempt to do so, of being too descriptive and not analytical enough, of arriving at muddled conclusions. Above all, however, according to Piven and Cloward, their critics are biased toward the privileged and powerful and thus have deliberately ignored, or downplayed, the crucial role of mass protest by the underclasses in securing welfare concessions. Relief expansiveness has not stemmed from the humanitarianism, or goodwill, of economic and political elites, as the critics allegedly claim, but rather from the aspirations of and periodic struggles by the common people against degradation and destitution, according to Piven and Cloward.

As already suggested, this book is not intended as a comprehensive, or even extensive, critique of *Regulating the Poor* or the entire social control thesis.[19] Rather, it is a brief, more modest work in which the contributors merely suggest that there are serious historical problems in attempting to explain American social welfare history, as they claim Piven and Cloward do, in some single, unchanging, almost mechanical fashion, to paraphrase from Raymond Mohl's essay—and which provides an opportunity for Piven and Cloward to respond to their critics, thus enriching debate on the issue. In the end, of course, readers will have to determine for themselves the credibility of the various contributors and the answers to the many questions raised in this work. Does rhetoric supersede fact and conception triumph over data in the essays and, if so, in which ones, in those by the critics, or in Piven and Cloward's response to them? Has the debate over social welfare and social control been miscast and, again, if so, by whom? Are the essayists apologists for the high and the mighty, as Piven and Cloward claim, or are Piven and Cloward guilty of oversimplifying history by singling out the role of the market economy in the making of welfare policy? Are the critics too insular and parochial in their approach, as Piven and Cloward contend, or are Piven and Cloward abusing history in an effort to alter society and perhaps even glorify their own careers, as one of the critics suggests? Are the contributors guilty of ignoring class consciousness and class conflict, as Piven and Cloward charge, or have Piven and Cloward exaggerated the influence of class in the American experience? To what extent has American social welfare policy been a product of benevolence and equalitarianism as opposed to self-interest and paternalism? To what degree has it been the result of uncertain and unanticipated factors, including political forces, as some of the critics contend, rather than a reasoned response to specific developments, as Piven and Cloward argue? Are human affairs too vagarious, disordered, and unstructured for us to be able to say something unshakable, and testable, about them, as several of the historians allege, or is history similar to the physical world—a determinate order about which statements that are certain, and predictable, can be concluded, as Piven and Cloward imply?

Whatever the answers to these (and other) questions, and regardless of who has gotten the upper hand in this exchange, Piven and Cloward clearly have made important scholarly contributions to social welfare history and the political economy of urban politics; they should be commended for, among other things, even attempting to develop a theoretical model with regard to these matters. Furthermore, although they were unable to attend the o.a.h. meeting when most of these papers were delivered orally, they were kind enough to take time from their busy schedules to reply to them in writing. Their response adds greatly to the usefulness of this work, and we thank them for it. It should be added, however, that the essayists have not seen that response and, of course, have not had the opportunity to reply to it.

Nevertheless, debates such as these, not only among academicians and their students but among practitioners and policy makers as well, certainly increase the level of our knowledge; perhaps some day they also will help improve the social welfare system — and ultimately the lives of the nation's needy citizens, Piven and Cloward's contentions notwithstanding. I am certain nothing would make them happier.

Milwaukee, Wisconsin   W.I.T.
May 1982

NOTES

1. In fact, all but two of the essays — the one by John Alexander and that by Frances Piven and Richard Cloward — were presented (in slightly different versions) at that session, held at the Hyatt Regency Hotel in San Francisco on 12 April 1980. I would like to take this opportunity to thank the Program Committee for the 1980 OAH Convention for approving the session, especially Linda Kerber, chair, and Louise Wade, a practitioner and strong supporter of social welfare history. I also would like to thank Professor Clarke A. Chambers of the University of Minnesota and Professor Reginald Horsman of the University of Wisconsin–Milwaukee for reading this introduction and suggesting ways to improve it; neither, of course, are responsible for any errors in fact, interpretation, or style, especially since I did not have the good sense to always take their advice.

2. Frances F. Piven and Richard A. Cloward, *Regulating the Poor: The Functions of Public Welfare* (New York: Pantheon, 1971).

3. A representative sample of such works includes Piven and Cloward, *Regulating the Poor;* Raymond Mohl, *Poverty in New York, 1783–1825* (New York: Oxford Univ. Press, 1971); Clifford Griffin, *Their Brother's Keeper: Moral Stewardship in the United States, 1800–1865* (New Brunswick, N.J.: Rutgers Univ. Press, 1965); Nathan Huggins, *Protestants Against Poverty: Boston's Charities, 1870–1900* (Westport, Conn.: Greenwood, 1971); Marvin Gettleman, "Charity and Social Classes in the United

States, 1874–1900," *American Journal of Economics and Sociology* 22 (April 1963), 313–30, (July 1963), 417–26, and "Philanthropy as Social Control in Late Nineteenth Century America: Some Hypotheses and Data on the Rise of Social Work," *Societas* 5 (Winter 1975), 49–59; Raymond Mohl and Neil Betten, "Paternalism and Pluralism: Immigrants and Social Welfare in Gary, Indiana, 1906–1940," *American Studies* 15 (Spring 1974), 5–30; Joseph Hawes, *Children in Urban Society: Juvenile Delinquency in Nineteenth Century America* (New York: Oxford Univ. Press, 1971); Steven Schlossman, *Love and the American Delinquent: The Theory and Practice of "Progressive" Juvenile Justice, 1825–1920* (Chicago: Univ. of Chicago Press, 1977); Anthony Platt, *The Child Savers: The Invention of Delinquency* (Chicago: Univ. of Chicago Press, 1965); Michael Katz, *The Irony of Early School Reform: Education Innovation in Mid-Nineteenth Century Massachusetts* (Cambridge, Mass.: Harvard Univ. Press, 1968); David Tyack, *The One Best System: A History of American Urban Education* (Cambridge, Mass.: Harvard Univ. Press, 1974); Stanley K. Schultz, *The Culture Factory: Boston Public Schools, 1789–1860* (New York: Oxford Univ. Press, 1973). Two other recent, although slightly different, works of this sort are Allan S. Horlick, *Country Boys and Merchant Princes: The Social Control of Young Men in New York* (Lewisburg, Pa.: Bucknell Univ. Press, 1975) and William Graebner, *A History of Retirement: The Meaning and Function of an American Institution, 1885–1978* (New Haven: Yale Univ. Press, 1980).

4. Willard Gaylin, Ira Glasser, Steven Marcus, and David Rothman, *Doing Good: The Limits of Benevolence* (New York: Pantheon, 1978), 83.

5. In addition to the Leiby essay, see Charles D. Cowager and Charles P. Atherton, "Social Control: A Rationale for Social Welfare," *Social Work* 19 (June 1974), 456–62, for a good discussion of social welfare and social control in its original sociological sense. Also see Morris Janowitz, "Social Control and Sociological Theory," *American Journal of Sociology* 18 (July 1975), 82–108, and *The Last Half-Century: Societal Change and Politics in America* (Chicago: Univ. of Chicago Press, 1978).

6. An earlier generation of American historians who wrote during the so-called Progressive Era—Frederick Jackson Turner, Charles A. Beard, Vernon L. Parrington, James Harvey Robinson, and others—called for a "New History" that would serve the present rather than the past. Also, like later members of the New Left, they tended to see politics as a conspiratorial process that masked the play of "real" forces, particularly social and economic ones. See John Higham, et al., *History* (Englewood Cliffs, N.J.: Prentice Hall, 1965), 104–31, 171–211; Robert Skotheim, *American Intellectual Histories and Historians* (Princeton: Princeton Univ. Press, 1966), 64–148; Charles Crowe, "Commentary on Progressive Histories," in *The Historian and the Climate of Opinion*, ed. by Robert Skotheim (Reading, Mass.: Addision-Wesley, 1969), 41–55. I should add that I am in no way implying that all those scholars who challenged the older, benign interpretation of the American past were members of the New Left.

7. See John Higham, "The Cult of the American Consensus," *Commentary* 27 (Feb. 1959), 93–100.

8. Most important were Gabriel Kolko, *Wealth and Power in America* (New York: Praeger, 1962); James N. Morgan, et al., *Income and Welfare in the United States* (New York: McGraw-Hill, 1962); Robert J. Lampman, *The Share of Top Wealth-Holders in National Wealth, 1922–1956* (Princeton: Princeton Univ. Press, 1962), and Herman P. Miller, *Rich Man, Poor Man* (New York: Crowell, 1964).

9. The literature on the New Left is enormous. Perhaps the best single work on its effect on the writing of American history, however, is Irwin Unger's "The 'New Left' and American History: Some Recent Trends in United States Historiography," *American Historical Review* 27 (July 1967), 1237–63.

10. Actually, thanks both to their writing — especially "The Weight of the Poor: A Strategy to End Poverty," *The Nation* 202 (2 May 1966), 510–17 — and to their role in helping to organize and actively participate in a number of grassroots protests by welfare recipients, they generally are considered to be among the founders and early theoreticians of that movement. At the time, both were on the faculty of the Columbia University School of Social Work.

11. *The Politics of Turmoil: Essays on Poverty, Race, and the Urban Crisis* (New York: Pantheon, 1974). Piven and Cloward's assumption was that a successful effort to arouse hundreds of thousands of poor people to demand relief for which they were eligible but for which they had not enrolled would, in the short run, provide direct financial aid to the poor and, in the long run, provoke such an acute fiscal crisis that government officials would be forced to launch some sort of national income maintenance program — or other meaningful reform.

12. Again, the assumption, of course, was that a capitalist regime will do nothing about poverty until its own interests are threatened; only when a large crisis occurs will it become responsive. Reform comes not from altruism but from pressure below.

13. *Poor People's Movements: Why They Succeed, How They Fail* (New York: Pantheon, 1977).

14. Piven and Cloward, *Regulating the Poor*, xiii. This notion about the cyclical nature of affairs can be found in the authors' later work as well: "Ordinarily, of course," they wrote in *Poor People's Movements,*

> elites do not support efforts to form organizations of lower-class people. But when insurgency wells up, apparently uncontrollable, elites respond. And one of their responses is to cultivate those lower class organizations which begin to emerge in such periods, for they have little to fear from organizations, especially from organizations which come to depend upon them for support. . . . When the tumult is over, these organizations usually fade, no longer useful to those who provided the resources necessary to their survival. Or the organization persists by becoming increasingly subservient to those on whom it depends. (p. xxii)

15. For a couple of the more critical early reviews, see Nathan Glazer, "Regulating the Poor, or Ruling Them?," *New York* (11 Oct. 1971), 55, and

Irving Kristol, "Welfare: The Best of Intentions, the Worst of Results," *Atlantic Monthly* 228 (17 Aug. 1971), 45.

16. Not only have more than two hundred thousand copies of the work been sold but it has also been reviewed in a wide variety of newspapers and such "popular" magazines as the *New York Times Book Review, The Nation,* the *New Republic, Atlantic Monthly, Saturday Review,* and others.

17. It was reviewed, however, in the leading scholarly journals in social welfare, sociology, economics, and political science, including, among others, the *Social Service Review, Social Work, American Journal of Sociology, Economist,* and the *Political Science Quarterly.*

18. Perhaps it would be appropriate to note here that after the completion of this manuscript a new book was published—James Patterson's *America's Struggle Against Poverty, 1900–1980* (Cambridge, Mass.: Harvard Univ. Press, 1981)— which, at times, analyzes *Regulating the Poor,* especially with regard to developments in the 1960s, and finds the Piven and Cloward thesis incorrect in several respects. Interested readers should consult that work—and Piven and Cloward's reaction to it, if and when it should appear.

19. Indeed, as readers will discover, several of the essayists have some sympathy for the social control thesis, but feel that it did not operate in the way in which Piven and Cloward claim.

THE FUNCTIONS OF PUBLIC WELFARE IN LATE-EIGHTEENTH-CENTURY PHILADELPHIA:

Regulating the Poor?

JOHN K. ALEXANDER
University of Cincinnati

Frances Fox Piven and Richard A. Cloward maintain, and correctly so, that the study of the functions of public welfare cannot be left solely to those "enmeshed" in the relief system. The danger is clear: all too often, such people feel they must justify the system. Piven and Cloward go even further in questioning the veracity of works on public relief. They contend most writers err by focusing on "morality" as the determining influence shaping public relief-giving. Because of these facts, the economic and political functions of public welfare, they argue, have been obscured. Their provocative and important *Regulating the Poor: The Functions of Public Welfare* is designed to set the record straight by showing how economic and political considerations can and have influenced the granting of public poor relief.[1]

The argument that one must be wary of the analyses produced by those enmeshed in the public welfare system is a sound one. But the argument cuts both ways. Piven and Cloward are themselves enmeshed in the system, albeit as critics who want to change the system. The authors candidly note that "much of our initial interest in public welfare arose during our association with Mobilization For Youth." They stress their own deep concern about how the system works by dedicating *Regulating the Poor* to "the welfare protest movement that arose in the 1960's; and to its leader, George A. Wiley." The notes on the authors make their own involvement clear: "Their articles in *The Nation* are widely credited with stimulating the formation of a grass-roots protest movement of welfare recipients."[2] Of course, Piven and Cloward may have arrived at their activist position only because of a detached and scholarly analysis. But their own activism gives added reason to scrutinize their analysis closely, for they were enmeshed in the public poor-relief system when their work was written.

One is tempted to question Piven and Cloward's analysis, in part, because of the extreme nature of the views they present.[3] If other writers have put too much emphasis on questions of morality, Piven and Cloward come close to dismissing moral considerations entirely. Why did the more prosperous citizens of early Lyons give charity to the needy? Because, say Piven and Cloward, they "sought to purchase their salvation through almsgiving"; such almsgiving "serve[d] a religious end for the prosperous."[4] And why did the older system that relied on church and private charity give way to a public system? Was it rooted in any kind of humanitarian concern for the poor? Of course not. "Several strains toward instability inherent in capitalist economies" made modern public relief systems necessary.[5] The historical evidence, claim Piven and Cloward, proves that public relief functions as a "mechanism" to meet the needs of "the market economy"; the historical evidence proves that public welfare has been used, and ruthlessly so, to serve the needs of "the larger economic and political order."[6]

Having labeled capitalism the villain of the piece, Piven and Cloward strive to show how capitalism dictated the specific workings of the public aid system. Capitalism produced periods of mass unemployment; "when mass unemployment leads to outbreaks of turmoil," relief programs are initiated or expanded "to mute civil disorder." When there is no mass unemployment, relief rolls are constricted "to reinforce work norms."[7] Thus public relief functions as the handmaiden of capitalism; the needs of the poor themselves are irrelevant. Of course, some public welfare programs, especially in the modern period, do benefit the needy. But benefiting the needy is *not* a real concern of those who direct the system. This can be seen, in part, by the fact that, according to Piven and Cloward, "under ordinary circumstances, . . . increases in unemployment do not produce comparable increases in the welfare rolls."[8]

Although Piven and Cloward were primarily concerned with the functioning of public relief in modern America, they sought to prove that the historical evidence showed that relief had always functioned in the way they claimed it had. But to build their case, Piven and Cloward drew their illustrations from other countries and from earlier historical periods.[9] Since *Regulating the Poor* focuses on the American public welfare system, it seems odd that the authors did not examine historical evidence from early America. This neglect cannot be attributed merely to the fact that the history of public welfare was not a well-explored topic when Piven and Cloward wrote. Several older, but still useful, works and some valuable historical studies of early American history published in the 1960s were available for their scrutiny.[10] Certainly the claims of Piven and Cloward should be tested with evidence drawn from earlier periods of American history as well as with evidence drawn from the earlier history of other countries. This essay offers one such test by examining the Piven and Cloward thesis in light of the public poor-relief system as it functioned in late-eighteenth-century Philadelphia.

Late-eighteenth-century Philadelphia offers a good locale for testing the Piven and Cloward thesis. Philadelphia was a growing, cosmopolitan, market city. From 1760 to 1800, the city's population increased approximately 350 percent; by 1800, almost 70,000 people, "thrown together from various quarters of the world," as William Smith said, called the city home.[11] As early as 1765, Lord Adam Gordon called Philadelphia "the first Town in America" and maintained it "bids fair to rival almost any in Europe."[12] And well he might. Philadelphia was the busiest port on the North American continent and it remained so until virtually the end of the century. In 1774 alone, 880 ships sailed into Philadelphia's harbor. By at least the 1770s, Philadelphia was also the leading manufacturing city of the British empire in the new world. Efforts to introduce the factory system met with only limited success in the last four decades of the century; nevertheless, increasing numbers of manufacturers and builders employed large numbers of workers as the period progressed. Equally important, over time, Philadelphia relied less and less on bound labor and moved, inexorably, toward a free-wage economic system. By the 1790s, labor unions came, however haltingly, onto the scene and work stoppages due to strikes occurred as employees struggled to raise their wages or improve their working conditions.[13]

Sam Bass Warner, whose work was available to Piven and Cloward, emphasized the capitalistic nature of late-eighteenth-century Philadelphia. He maintained that Philadelphians of that day shared in "the general American secular celebration of privatism," which held that "the individual should seek happiness in personal independence and in the search for wealth." "The popular goal of Philadelphia," said Warner, "was the individual race for wealth."[14] Warner may have overstated the case, but his analysis clearly shows that Philadelphia was a capitalistic, market city on the march. If the Piven and Cloward thesis holds for any early American area, it should hold for Philadelphia.

It is possible to find historical evidence drawn from Philadelphia that seems, at least indirectly, to support *aspects* of the Piven and Cloward thesis. In 1779, the city experienced what a contemporary called "the most alarming insurrection it had ever felt." The actions of greedy merchant capitalists were a prime cause of this crisis. These people manipulated prices in a way that threatened to destroy the ability of the lower orders to survive. Driven to what one of their leaders called desperation, militiamen took to the streets on October 4 to oppose price manipulation. They arrested four men and paraded them through the streets. The militia wound up in a bloody fight with persons who felt the militia intended to arrest them or to harm their friends. Six or seven people were killed; over a score were seriously wounded. Many citizens feared that yet more violence and bloodshed would follow. Although the civil disorder of 1779 apparently was not caused by mass unemployment, the situation comes close to fitting the Piven and Cloward model. The government responded rather weakly, but basically in the way Piven and Cloward said it would. Bypassing the regular public relief system, the state government quickly moved to distribute flour to the people. (A special preference was given to militiamen who agreed to leave the city due to a call-up requested by George Washington.) This initiation of a new form of public relief was supported by a private citizen's call to raise charity monies for the poor and distressed of the city.[15] In this instance, the expansion of aid clearly seems to have been based on a desire, as Piven and Cloward said, to mute civil disorder.

One can also build a case to show that poor relief in Philadelphia, both public *and* private, was often designed to control the poor. And one goal may well have been to prevent civil disorder.[16] But even if these points are correct, they offer only minimal support for the Piven and Cloward thesis. Piven and Cloward do not argue that poor relief was used in some general way as a mechanism of socioeconomic control and possibly to prevent civil disorder. Rather, they tie the functionings of public relief directly to the problems supposedly caused by capitalism. They hold that public assistance was expanded after mass unemployment caused disorder, or alternatively, was contracted to reinforce work norms. Piven and Cloward would have been on far safer ground had they maintained that welfare was often used to try to control the poor in a variety of ways. But they were determined to indict capitalism and, in so doing, walked into swampy ground dotted with patches of quicksand.

One major problem with the Piven and Cloward argument is that it too facilely bypasses the role of private relief in earlier periods. Private poor relief was an integral and major part of the welfare structure of late-eighteenth-century Philadelphia. At times public relief was actually dependent on private aid. In 1765, over 25 percent of the public funds expended to maintain the poor came from private donations to the overseers of the poor who were strapped for funds. From 1766 to 1788, the public relief system of the city was, in fact, legally directed by a private charity organization. Churches maintained their own welfare systems, and the Quakers even maintained their own almshouse. Mutual aid organizations provided assistance to individual groups. Ethnic organizations and a wide variety of other private organizations offered help to the needy. Innumerable ad hoc subscription groups provided benefits for those reduced to destitution because of various misfortunes such as harsh winters, natural disasters, or epidemic sickness.[17] The private charity network was so vast and so impressive that, in 1787, the public relief officials actually complained their job was made harder because Philadelphia had so many charities that the needy of other areas flocked to the city.[18] The extent of such private charity was, at times, staggering. In the severe winter of 1761-62, a private subscription fund provided aid to about one in ten Philadelphians. A similar fund in 1783-84, which aided the laboring poor, provided relief to about one in seven Philadelphians.[19] Because this private relief structure existed, the efforts of public officials to control the amount of relief given could be subverted. And if the public welfare system could not control the expansion and contraction of poor relief, the Piven and Cloward analysis becomes questionable.

Some of the private aid given in the Philadelphia of that earlier day was, despite what Piven and Cloward imply, rooted in a simple humanitarian concern for the poor.[20] To say this is not necessarily to maintain that such assistance was, to use Piven and Cloward's term, based solely on morality. Indeed, private charity grew from a complex set of roots, and humanitarianism was but one of them.

The extensive network of private charity was based in part on the fact that Philadelphians believed they lived in a world marked by instability. It was often stated that misfortune could easily plummet anyone from prosperity to adversity, and even to debtors' prison. Philadelphians knew only too well that "diseases and death . . . are secretly lurking everywhere" and that a range of natural disasters could leave one destitute.[21] Given such dangers, it is understandable why public calls for charity routinely proclaimed, "It is a prudent foresight of the disasters which may happen to our selves, which induces us to assist others: that they may be willing to return the favor to us on a similar occasion." Thus, the idea of charity as insurance formed an organic part of the whole scheme of private poor relief.[22] As the theme of charity as insurance suggests, private charity could be shaped by something more than simple morality and yet not be designed merely to meet problems caused by capitalism.

Private relief also was often rooted in a desire to control as well as to relieve the poor. The aid given to relieve seasonal or other forms of unemployment may well have been designed, in part, to prevent civil disorder. For example, in 1798 when yellow fever threw many out of work, private charity, aided by grants from the government, relieved the distressed. But careful efforts were made to control the poor and to see that they did not cause problems. People who moved out of Philadelphia to obtain relief in a tent city were told to be orderly, and armed guards patrolled to see that order was maintained. A Philadelphian of the day noted the value of such actions when he said the assistance provided was valuable not simply because it relieved the poor but also because it preserved their "morals."[23] But if some private and government aid was designed, in part, to *prevent* civil disorder, that is something quite different than what Piven and Cloward claimed was the case. Moreover, massive private poor relief, at times supplemented by government funds, was often called into existence due to the immediate need of the people for relief, not as a response to outbreaks of civil disorder.[24]

Although one must give some attention to private poor relief because it was so important in early Philadelphia, Piven and Cloward analyze public relief. Their thesis, therefore, deserves to be examined primarily in light of Philadelphia's public poor-relief system. Such an examination shows that Piven and Cloward's view runs counter to the great bulk of historical evidence.

If Piven and Cloward are correct, expansions of the public welfare rolls or initiation of public welfare programs occurred as a response to civil disorder caused by mass unemployment. Philadelphia experienced two major expansions of its welfare system in the last four decades of the eighteenth century. Neither was brought about because of civil disorder caused by mass unemployment. The first major expansion in the city's public poor-relief system took place in the 1760s and came about because the older system could not meet its legally mandated duties. The problems that led to this expansion, which initiated a new program, had built up over a long period.

When the first Pennsylvania legislature met in 1682, it mandated that "if any person or persons shall fall into Decay and poverty, and not be able to maintain themselves and children, with their honest Endeavors," the county justices were to "make provision for them." In addition, the County Court was thereafter to see that "Care be taken for their future comfortable subsistence." The next year, the Provincial Council struck the same theme when it said provision should be made "for the Sustenance of the People," so "that there may be Care taken Every one may partake." Pennsylvania's government thus declared that the poor should be maintained, and that principle remained a part of the colony's law even as the structure of public poor relief was altered.[25]

By 1700, public poor relief in Philadelphia was in the hands of overseers of the poor. In 1706, this office was written into law with the overseers being appointed by the county justices to serve one-year terms. The overseers were authorized to collect the poor tax and to maintain the poor. In this early period, the overseers had a very difficult time raising the money needed to maintain the poor. Part of the problem apparently stemmed from the fact that needy people from other areas went into Philadelphia to obtain relief. The legislature helped the city deal with this problem in 1718 by defining what constituted a legal settlement, which entitled people to receive welfare from a given locality.[26] But the difficulty of relieving the poor continued, and the city, it appears, looked to the creation of an almshouse to lessen the costs. By 1732, the almshouse was in operation, but it had not helped reduce the cost of maintaining the poor. According to the Philadelphia Common Council, the new almshouse "in no wise contribute[s] to Lessen s[ai]d [poor] Taxes." Although the legislature, in 1735, allowed the overseers to raise the poor tax, they continued to find it most difficult to make ends meet.[27]

The endemic economic problems of the Philadelphia overseers may well have made it impossible for them to comply with a 1749 law that in itself challenges the Piven and Cloward thesis. That law directed the overseers to provide various cloth materials to "poor persons" who were "likely to become chargeable for want of employment, and to employ such persons in manufacturing the same, and to make them reasonable allowance for their labor."[28] Given this law, the poor were to be provided with employment; yet Piven and Cloward said that providing relief due to ordinary unemployment was *not,* and is not, a feature of public relief.

The problems of just keeping the public welfare system working reached crisis proportions by the early 1760s. The poor taxes were high and growing higher. The number of poor was increasing; the almshouse was ridiculously overcrowded. In 1764, the overseers made a bold move to deal with their manifold problems. They asked the legislature to create a house of employment and offered the rationale that three-fourths of the poor maintained by the city could earn enough in the summer to see them through the winter if set to work in such an institution. The overseers renewed their request in 1766 and argued that even with repeated poor taxes, and even though citizens had donated one-third as much as was raised by the poor tax, there was not money enough to support the public relief system. Other groups supported the overseers' request.[29]

The legislature responded to these pleas by authorizing creation of a house of employment. The house was to be financed by a private group called "the Contributors to the Relief and Employment of the Poor within the City of Philadelphia." Once the house was built, the contributors would annually elect persons from their number to be managers of the house. The managers took over the overseers' duty of determining how much poor tax to request to maintain the poor. The managers also were to determine how the bulk of the poor tax should be spent. The office of overseer was retained, but the duties were legally reduced to collecting taxes, removing non-resident poor, and providing short-term assistance.[30] The 1766 legislation thus created a mixed private-public system of public poor relief.

The house of employment, which opened its doors in 1767, was designed to assist the poor and also, it was hoped, to reduce the cost of poor relief.[31] One way, it was thought, to reduce costs was to unite all of greater Philadelphia into a single system. This was done. One goal was to reduce costly battles over legal settlement and yet to provide aid to those who clearly lived in the city but lacked a legal residence due to moving about in the greater Philadelphia area.[32] In addition, it was believed that putting public poor relief under one set of managers would make it "as cheap and convenient . . . as possible." Costs also would be reduced because the poor able to work would labor in the house of employment. The 1749 ideal of providing work for those who faced unemployment was also retained. The legislature directed that all poor persons who offered to work "for their maintenance" were to be employed "at such wages, that their labor will contribute to the advancement of the design of the said [Contributorship] corporation."[33]

There can be no question that the creation of the house of employment initiated a new public poor-relief program. It also marked an expansion in the relief rolls, for far more people could be and were maintained in the house of employment than could be or were maintained in the old almshouse.[34] But these changes were not brought about because mass unemployment in the period 1764–66 produced outbreaks of civil disorder. Rather, the evidence shows that the changes occurred because the old system had become both inadequate and outrageously expensive. The government officials may have been more concerned about reducing costs than they were about helping the poor, but the evidence does not support the Piven and Cloward argument that expansion of the welfare rolls and innovation in programs happened because mass unemployment caused civil disorder.[35]

The second major expansion of public poor relief took place in the last years of the century. Between 1794 and 1796, the yearly average number of people in the house hovered around 380. In 1796–97, the average jumped to 417; then the explosion occurred. In the last three years of the century, the average number in the house went from 508 to 605 to 699.[36] Mass unemployment did not cause outbreaks of civil disorder during these years. Why then did the explosion happen? It came about because the city's population had grown dramatically. In 1790, slightly more than 42,500 people lived in Philadelphia. Yellow fever epidemics of the 1790s killed thousands of people; yet by 1800 the census recorded the city's population as 67,811. Clearly the city had experienced incredible growth, and most of that growth appears to have taken place during the last half of the 1790s. Thus the dramatic expansion of relief seems to have been caused by population increase. As a contemporary observer noted, the number of poor had "greatly multiplied with the increased population of the State."[37]

The one truly drastic contraction of the public welfare rolls that

occurred in the last four decades of the eighteenth century in Philadelphia cannot be explained by the Piven and Cloward thesis. Certainly the public poor-relief officials did not seek the major contraction. At various times during the American Revolution, both the
British and American armies took over part or all of the house of
employment. Poor taxes, never easy to garner, became impossible
to collect. In fact, the welfare officials were reduced to borrowing
and even begging for funds. Thus the war itself caused the contraction.[38] This one example does not, however, disprove Piven and
Cloward's argument on contraction. The desire to reinforce work
norms may have produced other less drastic contractions in the rolls.

The Piven and Cloward thesis on contraction seems, at first glance,
to gain support when one examines the actions and attitudes of the
contributorship managers in regard to outdoor relief and reform of
the poor. In June 1769, the managers told the overseers that outdoor relief should stop and that persons entitled to the benefit of
the house "shall be obliged to remove therein, and be subject to the
Laws and Ordinances for the government of the same."[39] The managers wanted the poor forced into the house in part to reform them.
In 1770, the managers claimed that many who entered the house had
"dissolute manners" and were "Nuisances to the Community." Put
to hard work and deprived of liquor, many had become "so remark-
edly Altered as to become subjects of Surprise to many of the Inhabitants who had known them in their former condition."[40] The
managers were clearly stressing a philosophy of reforming the dregs of
society, which is something rather different than merely enforcing
work norms. The managers were, it appears, looking to long-term
results rather than just responding to the immediate employment situation. The difference between that and what Piven and Cloward
maintain should have happened is important. It is also vital to note
that the managers, with only a few exceptions, tried to enforce the
rule against outdoor relief for as long as the contributorship lasted.[41]
Given Piven and Cloward's conclusions, the employment situation
should have dictated whether the managers supported or opposed
outdoor relief. But there was good reason for the managers rather
constantly to oppose outdoor pensions, and that reason had nothing
at all to do with the rates of employment in Philadelphia. Even before
the doors of the house opened, the contributorship had run deeply
into debt. The economic situation grew steadily worse. Part of the
problem was that the poor who labored in the house simply could

not generate enough income to justify the high cost of running the house. Because of this, the managers wanted to reduce overseer expenditures as much as possible. Moreover, because the economic problems steadily worsened, the managers quickly came under and remained under public attack. Thus, the managers' continuing efforts to eliminate outdoor relief were probably sparked as much by economic necessity as by the desire to reform the poor.[42]

Even though the contributorship managers wanted to reform the dissolute, they also responded to ordinary unemployment in a way that challenges the Piven and Cloward view. As noted, Piven and Cloward maintain that "under ordinary circumstances, . . . increases in unemployment do not produce comparable increases in the welfare rolls." But, at least in the period before the Revolutionary War, the contributorship managers did *routinely* expand the welfare rolls in the winter when the poor found it difficult to procure employment.[43] For example, in January 1770 the managers observed that in the preceding year the average number of people in the house from April to October was 250 and from October to April, 320. The records of the number of poor in the house in 1771–72 show the standard trend. In June and July 1771, the number in the house was between 302 and 304. By December the total had shot up to 402, and in January and February between 416 and 418 poor people resided in the house.[44] The records for the period 1780 to 1788 are not as complete as those for the earlier period. Thus one cannot say with absolute assurity that the later contributorship managers routinely followed the earlier practice. But the available evidence suggests that was the case. In March 1786, the managers noted that many in the house had been examined and found "fit to be discharged and provide for themselves." But the managers were convinced that "from the General Stagnation of Business and Want of usual Employment at this Season of the Year," the poor "Cannot procure Work." The "Principles of Humanity," said the managers, caused them to judge it improper to turn these people out. The same pattern was followed in 1787; during the winter months the number of persons in the house increased. In 1788, the managers struck the same themes stated in 1786 when they noted that, despite orders to reduce the house's population, the number of inhabitants remained high. This was the case even though "a considerable Number" of the poor were "deemed fit to be turned out to get their livelihood as they could." The fact was that "from the uncommon Rigour of the Weather at this season and

the general scarcity, or indeed stagnation of Employment[,] we have
been able to get rid but of very few from here." The managers later
noted that the rolls had indeed been expanded during the winter. For
the year ending in April 1788, an average of 336 people had been
maintained in the house. But, during the preceding severe winter,
the average was upwards of 400, and in the middle of March there
were 460 people in the house. At times, the managers were also willing to expand or contract outdoor relief based on the ordinary employment situation. In 1786, the managers eliminated pension aid
in the summer and reinstituted it as winter approached.[45] Thus, even
when anxious to reduce the cost of public relief, the contributorship
managers expanded the rolls to meet seasonal unemployment.

Even considering the contributorship managers' desire to see that
the "dissolute" poor were reformed in the house, the historical evidence concerning the contributorship managers does not support the
Piven and Cloward thesis. That thesis is challenged even more when
one examines the attitudes and actions of the overseers of the poor
under the contributorship. The overseers consistently rejected the
managers' efforts to reduce or eliminate outdoor relief. The overseers
argued that it made no economic sense to force all poor people into
the house, and they offered telling examples that proved their case.
In addition, they contended that it would be cruel and unfair to force
all impoverished persons into the house. Equally important, the overseers simply continued to grant outdoor relief no matter what the
managers or the law dictated; since the overseers collected the poor
tax, they could and did spend money on outdoor assistance throughout the contributorship period. These practices produced protracted
battles between the overseers and the managers.[46] And the actions
of the overseers demonstrate that Piven and Cloward were simply
wrong when they claimed that "relief practice is always more restrictive than relief law."[47]

By stridently supporting outdoor relief, the overseers showed real
concern for the needy. But something more than morality prompted
them to champion such relief. If the managers had their way, the
overseers would be reduced to being mere tax collectors and agents
to determine where the poor had a legal settlement. The overseers
resented the effort to reduce their power, in part because they wanted
to exercise some discretionary power. The overseers did not want
to serve merely as underlings of the managers. A group of overseers
openly stated this when they maintained the battles between the man-

agers and overseers could be traced to "too great an ostentation of superiority" on the part of the managers and "too great a degree of Jealousy" on the part of the overseers. Given this analysis, the manager-overseer battles over outdoor relief sprang as much from concerns about wielding power as from any philosophical differences on what public welfare should or should not do.[48] This evidence again presents a picture that, while not necessarily flattering to officials, is simply not consistent with the Piven and Cloward argument.

Although the contributorship managers and the overseers had sharp disagreements, they did agree on at least two vital points that further question the Piven and Cloward view. First, it was clear to these officials that the public welfare system was in deep financial trouble. Because of this, the officials had to struggle just to keep the system running. They did not have the financial power necessary to expand the system significantly. For the Piven and Cloward thesis to hold, the public relief officials had to agree on what relief should do *and* they also had to have the power to change the system. That power was largely lacking in Philadelphia.[49] Second, the managers and overseers, as much as the evidence allows us to tell, agreed that assistance *should* be expanded when unemployment expanded. We have already seen this view expressed and acted upon by the contributorship managers. The overseers, in addition to championing regular outdoor relief, argued that the public poor-relief officials should "at all Times [be] ready to give Employment to such Paupers as make Application for Relief on Account of the Failure of Employers, which is either the real or pretended Cause of a large Proportion of those who, the Public are obliged to assist."[50] This view is, of course, just the opposite of what Piven and Cloward said it would be.

By using a technicality in the poor laws, the overseers were able to overthrow the contributorship in 1788. This put public poor relief solely in the hands of appointed public officials, now called the guardians of the poor.[51] Given the overseers' stress on aiding rather than reforming the poor, it is no surprise that the guardians quickly asked the legislature to insure that the house function as a house of refuge for the "orderly & respectable Poor who go in for Relief & Employment," not as an institution to reform "immoral[,] loose & abandoned people." The legislature agreed. In 1789, it ordered that disorderly people no longer be sent, as they had been under the contributorship, to the house. The legislature proclaimed the house should exist "for the accommodation of the poor and the infirm and not for the reformation of the idle and profligate."[52]

Although the guardians were anxious to make the house a house of refuge, they had another pressing concern. They admitted they had led the citizens of Philadelphia to believe that they could, if given control of the house, lower the poor tax. The new guardian managers of the house put the problem squarely: "*it now rests solely on us* to perform that which We gave the Public expectation was our Object and on the *Event* is our *Reputation at stake.*" If the guardians failed to lower the cost of public poor relief, "what a Clamour will there be raised against us! and what matter of Triumph will it afford to those who have opposed our Measures!"[53] These officials, it is clear, were as concerned with protecting their reputations as they were with possibly using public poor relief to meet the needs of a capitalistic system.

Clamors were raised against the guardians and they desperately tried to keep down costs, to no avail.[54] Even given their concern with reputation, the guardians, like the contributorship managers before them, routinely expanded the relief rolls to meet ordinary problems of unemployment. Under the guardians, the number of people in the house rose during winter seasons when employment opportunities declined. For example, in June and July 1794 the house contained between 298 and 313 people. By December, 366 people were in the house, and the number jumped to 449 in January 1795 and then to 461 in February.[55] In 1793, the guardians did declare that regular outdoor pensions would no longer be given. But outdoor relief other than pensions was still to be given and, as in years gone by, even the ban against regular pensions was not strictly followed.[56] Thus the guardians continued to expand the relief rolls merely to meet the ordinary problems of unemployment, and outdoor relief was, as it had been, dispensed regularly.

When the guardians decided that programs should be initiated, they also did something that challenges the Piven and Cloward thesis. In March 1789, the guardians agreed that they should establish a foundling hospital for children, "unnaturally deserted in infancy by their Parents." Writing in their own records and not for public consumption, they said that "Humanity" required this innovation. The fact was, they maintained, such children "could never have offended Society" and, thus, "have the first Claim on us."[57] It again seems that something other than civil disorder caused by mass unemployment could lead to a desire to initiate welfare programs in Philadelphia.

One does not have to go to the extreme of saying the guardians always acted from motives of simple humanitarianism. The guardian managers, like the contributorship managers before them, came to believe that many of the house's residents could and should be reformed through hard work and deferential behavior.[58] The guardians also proudly noted the house was the biggest hospital in the city as well as a place of refuge. When attacked for the high cost of poor relief, defenders of the guardians, possibly guardians themselves, asserted that "the Alms House may now more properly be called an Infirmary, than a House of Employment." While carefully noting it had become a hospital "out of absolute necessity," defenders of the house's hospital function noted "with pride" that the house was well on the way to becoming a medical school. Indeed, it would soon rival the "very best" such institutions, and great doctors and surgeons would "proudly" work at the house.[59] The guardians seemed to want to gain reputation as well as to save it. Certainly one must note that matters of personal pride were often very important to the public relief officials. This as much as a humanitarian concern for the poor and a desire to reform some of them may have guided the guardians' actions. Once again the evidence suggests that the Piven and Cloward thesis does not explain what happened under the guardianship system of public poor relief in Philadelphia.

The history of public poor relief in late-eighteenth-century Philadelphia obviously is complex. Private poor relief was so important a component of the welfare structure that the public officials could not effectively control the expansion or contraction of poor relief, even had they wished to do so. The officials did work to provide assistance during ordinary periods of unemployment. Innovations and expansion of the poor-relief rolls did occur when there was no civil disorder caused by mass unemployment. Throughout the period, public officials had to struggle just to keep the system creaking along. Dramatic changes in the level of poor relief, thus, were very difficult to achieve. The contributorship managers did try to curtail or eliminate outdoor relief, but they did not do this just to reinforce work norms. The desire to eliminate or to curtail outdoor relief sprang from a variety of reasons. The managers had to try to reduce the poor tax. They wanted to reform the "dissolute." In the main wealthier and from a higher socio-economic class than the overseers, they wanted to dictate how the system would work.[60] The overseers, jealous of the managers, wanted to hold a public post that gave them a sense of status. Thus, the system functioned as it did in part because the managers and overseers wanted to wield power. The system also may have functioned to control the poor in ways that do not match the specific thesis advanced by Piven and Cloward. Still, humanitarian concern for the needy was a part of the functioning of public welfare. Despite all the complexities, this much is clear: the Piven and Cloward thesis does not accurately depict the functioning of Philadelphia's public welfare system.

The historical evidence from Philadelphia is, of course, only part of the story of public poor relief even in late-eighteenth-century America.[61] And while the Piven and Cloward thesis does not hold for Philadelphia, perhaps it accurately describes the functioning of public welfare in other American areas at other times. Only careful and close analysis can determine if that is the case.

NOTES

1. *Regulating the Poor: The Functions of Public Welfare* (New York: Pantheon, 1971), xvi.

2. Ibid., v, vii. The notes on the authors appear in the Vintage Books edition (New York, 1972).

3. In addition to the illustrations in the text, note that the authors say the violence of 1932 "signaled political disaffection on a scale unparalleled in the American experience" (*Regulating the Poor,* 68). This claim seems ludicrous when one considers the political disaffection that caused the American Revolution and the American Civil War.

4. Ibid., 10.

5. Ibid., 3–11, 16, 21 with quotation at p. 4.

6. Ibid., xiii–xvii with quotations at pp. xiii, xvii.

7. Ibid., xiii, 3.

8. Ibid., 341 for the quotation; on benefits see p. xiv.

9. Ibid., xv and cf. 3–41.

10. See, for example, David M. Schneider, *The History of Public Welfare in New York State 1609–1866* (Chicago: Univ. of Chicago Press, 1938); Charles Lawrence, *History of the Philadelphia Almshouses and Hospitals* (Philadelphia: C. Lawrence,1905); Robert W. Kelso, *The History of Public Relief in Massachusetts 1620–1920* (Boston: Houghton Mifflin, 1920); Raymond A. Mohl, "Poverty in Early America, a Reappraisal: The Case of Eighteenth-Century New York City," *New York History* 50 (Jan. 1969), 5–27; various works cited by Raymond A. Mohl in "Poverty, Pauperism, and Social Order

in the Preindustrial American City, 1780–1840," *Social Science Quarterly* 52 (March 1972), 934-48.

11. Quotation cited in Carl and Jessica Bridenbaugh, *Rebels and Gentlemen: Philadelphia in the Age of Franklin* (New York: Reynal and Hitchcock, 1942), 16; the population figures are from John K. Alexander, "The Philadelphia Numbers Game: An Analysis of Philadelphia's Eighteenth-Century Population," *Pennsylvania Magazine of History and Biography* 97 (July 1974), 324, and *Return of the whole number of persons . . . for the second census . . . One Thousand Eight Hundred* (Washington, D.C.: Apollo Press, 1802), 49.

12. Newton D. Mereness, ed., *Travels in the American Colonies* (New York: Antiquarian Press, 1916), 411.

13. John K. Alexander, "'A Year . . . Famed in the Annals of History': Philadelphia in 1776" in *Philadelphia 1776-2076: A Three Hundred Year View,* ed. by Dennis J. Clark (Port Washington, N.Y.: Kennikat, 1975), 8-9; Sharon V. Salinger, "Under One Roof: Artisans and the Transformation of Labor in Late 18th-Century Philadelphia," a paper presented at the 1980 meeting of the American Historical Association, Washington, D.C.; Sharon V. Salinger, "Colonial Labor in Transition: The Decline of Indentured Servitude in Late Eighteenth-Century Philadelphia," *Labor History* 22 (Spring 1981), 165-91.

14. *The Private City: Philadelphia in Three Periods of Its Growth* (Philadelphia: Univ. of Pennsylvania Press, 1968), 3-45, with quotations at pp. 3, 45.

15. In a long statement of their grievances issued in May 1779, militiamen did note that "many of us are at a loss to this day what Course or Station of Life to adopt to Support ourselves and Families." This comment suggests employment problems troubled militiamen. But their statement clearly focused on price manipulation and other problems not associated with issues of employment. See *Pennsylvania Archives, First Series,* 12 vols. (Philadelphia: Joseph Severns & Co., 1852–56), 7: 392-95 with quotation at p. 393. On the events of 1779, see John K. Alexander, "The Fort Wilson Incident of 1779: A Case Study of the Revolutionary Crowd," *William and Mary Quarterly,* 3d ser., 31 (Oct. 1974), 589-612, with quotation at p. 590; "Plan," *Pennsylvania Packet,* 12 Oct. 1779.

16. These points are developed at length in John K. Alexander, *Render Them Submissive: Responses to Poverty in Philadelphia, 1760-1800* (Amherst: Univ. of Massachusetts Press, 1980), especially 86-169.

17. Ibid., 87-90, 110-11, 122-41.

18. "The Remonstrance and Petition of the Managers elected by the Contributors to the relief and Employment of the Poor in the City of Philadelphia &ca and the Overseers of the Poor of the said City and districts Connected therewith [21 November 1787]," Records of the General Assembly, General Assembly file, Record Group 7, Box 2, Pennsylvania State Archives, Harrisburg.

19. Alexander, *Render Them Submissive,* 9.

20. For example, see ibid., 124-27.

21. "Monitor," *Pennsylvania Packet,* 17 March 1790; see also "Benevo-

lence," ibid., 17 August 1787; John H. Powell, *Bring Out Your Dead: The Great Plague of Yellow Fever in Philadelphia in 1793* (Philadelphia: Univ. of Pennsylvania Press, 1949); "To do good," *Aurora,* 9 July 1796; "Philanthropos," *Pennsylvania Journal,* 22 June 1774.

22. "Humanity," *Philadelphia Minerva,* 2 Jan. 1796; "Pity," *ibid.,* 27 Jan. 1798; "Charity," *Carey's Pennsylvania Evening Herald,* 28 April 1787; see also the sources cited in preceding note.

23. "A Friend to Merit," *Porcupine's Gazette,* 15 Oct. 1798, and Thomas Condie and Robert Folwell, *History of the Pestilence, commonly called yellow fever, which almost desolated Philadelphia in the months of August, September & October, 1798* (Philadelphia: F. Folwell, 1799).

24. In addition to the items already cited, see, for example, *Independent Gazetteer,* 31 Dec. 1785; *Pennsylvania Gazette,* 18 April 1791 and 3 Oct. 1797; *Federal Gazette,* 12 Jan. 1799.

25. George Staughton, Benjamin M. Nead, and Thomas McCamant, eds., *Charter to William Penn, and Laws of the Province of Pennsylvania, Passed between the years 1682 and 1700* . . . (Harrisburg: Hart, 1879), 115, and *Minutes of the Provincial Council of Pennsylvania* . . . 16 vols. (Philadelphia and Harrisburg; Theo. Fenn & Co., 1838–53), 1:78.

26. *Minutes of the Provincial Council,* 2:9–10, 407–10; *Minutes of the Common Council of the City of Philadelphia, 1704 to 1776* (Philadelphia: Crissy & Markley, 1847), 13, 17, 34, 80, 83, 116, 141, 159; J.T. Mitchell and Henry Flanders, eds., *The Statutes at Large of Pennsylvania from 1682 to 1801,* 15 vols. (Harrisburg: C. M. Busch, 1896-1911), 2: 251–54; 3: 221–25.

27. *Minutes of the Common Council,* 309, 330, 332, 396–97, 398–99 with quotation at p. 330; *Statutes at Large,* 4:266–77.

28. *Statutes at Large,* 5: 79–86 with quotation at p. 85.

29. Minutes of the Managers' of the House of Employment for 1769–78, 31 (hereafter Managers' Minutes, 1769–78), Philadelphia City and County Archives, Philadelphia (hereafter PCA); and *Pennsylvania Archives, Eighth Series,* 8 vols. (Harrisburg: Bureau of Publications, 1931–35), 7:5506, 5535–36, 5538ff., 5694, 5738, 5823–24, 5830–31; Gary B. Nash, "Poverty and Poor Relief in Pre-Revolutionary Philadelphia," *William and Mary Quarterly,* 3d ser., 33 (Jan. 1976), 6–11, 17–20.

30. *Statutes at Large,* 7:9–17 with quotation at p. 10. The house of employment was actually two institutions in one building. The east wing, or almshouse section, housed those who could not labor; the west wing, or house of employment section, housed those who could work and those confined because they were disorderly and likely to become public charges. Since the term *house of employment* was standardly used to refer to the whole institution, I shall follow that practice.

31. See sources in note 29; "W.R.," *Pennsylvania Gazette,* 9 Jan. 1773; Managers' Minutes, 1769–78, 226–33.

32. *Pennsylvania Archives, Eighth Series,* 7:6148. The creation of a greater Philadelphia system angered many people outside the city and produced efforts to alter the system. See Alexander, *Render Them Submissive,* 90, 106, 115–16.

33. *Pennsylvania Archives, Eighth Series,* 7:6148, and *Statutes at Large,* 7: 15.

34. Managers' Minutes, 1769–78, 231–33, and see also sources cited in note 36.

35. For a general indictment of the house system, see "Memorial," *Aurora,* 28 July 1796.

36. Managers of the Alms House Minutes for 1788–96, 454, 499, PCA (hereafter Managers' Minutes, 1788–96) and Minutes of the Managers of the Almshouse for 1796–1803, 8 and entries of 24 April 1797, 14 May 1799, 7 May 1800, PCA (hereafter Managers' Minutes, 1796–1803).

37. Quotation from *Gazette of the United States,* 8 Sept. 1796; for the population figures see sources in note 11.

38. Alexander, *Render Them Submissive,* 104–5.

39. Managers' Minutes, 1769–78, 8–9.

40. Ibid., 32–33.

41. When the managers did accept outdoor relief they seemed to do it primarily to reduce the friction between them and the overseers. See Alexander, *Render Them Submissive,* 90–97, 100–101, 106–10.

42. See, for example, *Pennsylvania Archives, Eighth Series,* 7: 6097–99, 6101, 6322–24; 8: 7402, 7421; Managers' Minutes, 1769–78, 124, 226–33; Managers of the Alms House Minutes for 1780–88, 18, 36–37, PCA (hereafter Managers' Minutes, 1780–88); "To the public," *Pennsylvania Packet,* 24 March 1787; "Half Earnest, " ibid., 11 Dec. 1788.

43. On unemployment caused by winter, see, for example, "A Friend," *Federal Gazette,* 7 April 1790; *Pennsylvania Packet,* 12 Jan. 1791; *Independent Gazetteer,* 31 Dec. 1785.

44. Managers' Minutes, 1769–78, 32–33, 99, 100, 118, 121, and passim.

45. Managers' Minutes, 1780–88, 46, 48, 55, 59, 67, 70, 71, 99, 102, 112 with quotations at pp. 46, 48, 99.

46. Alexander, *Render Them Submissive,* 90–97, 100–101, 105–11, 114–15.

47. Piven and Cloward, *Regulating the Poor,* 147.

48. Managers' Minutes, 1788–96, 80. See also citation in note 46.

49. See notes 38, 42, 45.

50. Rough Minutes of the City Board of the Overseers of the Poor and Guardians of the Poor for 1787–96, letter to managers filed with entry of 28 Feb. 1788, PCA (hereafter Rough Minutes).

51. Alexander, *Render Them Submissive,* 105–6, 110–11.

52. Managers' Minutes, 1788–96, 86, and *Statutes at Large,* 13: 254.

53. Managers' Minutes, 1788–96, 53, 54.

54. Ibid., 52–54, 233–34, 430, 453–54, 462, 498, 500, 502; Minutes of the General Board of the Guardians of the Poor for 1788–95, entries of 25 Nov. 1793, 3 Feb., 2 March, 2 June, 1 Sept., 6 Oct. 1794, PCA (hereafter General Board Minutes); Managers' Minutes, 1796–1803, 7–8, 10–11, entries of 14 May 1798, 22 May 1799, 7 May 1800; "Half Earnest," *Pennsylvania Packet,* 11 Dec. 1788.

55. Managers' Minutes, 1788–96, 499, and for similar shifts in population in other years see 113, 231, 318, 389, 454; Managers' Minutes, 1796–1803, 8, entries of 24 April 1797, 14 May 1798, 22 May 1799, 7 May 1800.

56. Rough Minutes, entries of 6 Dec. 1793, 5 June 1794, 23 April 1795.

57. General Board Minutes, 25, 32–33. It is not clear if the foundling hospital was established; but, as noted below in the text, the house did come to serve a major hospital function.

58. Alexander, *Render Them Submissive,* 119–20.

59. "Charitas," *Gazette of the United States,* 11 July 1799, and "No. II," ibid., 23 July 1799.

60. Alexander, *Render Them Submissive,* 92–93, 111–14.

61. Raymond A. Mohl's study of public relief as it functioned in eighteenth-century New York City criticizes that system, but stresses that poor relief in the city was guided by a humanitarian concern for the poor. See Mohl, *Poverty in New York, 1783–1825* (New York: Oxford, 1971), 12–13, 37–51, 66–67, 159–64.

THE ABOLITION OF PUBLIC OUTDOOR RELIEF,
1870-1900:
A Critique of the Piven and Cloward Thesis

RAYMOND A. MOHL
Florida Atlantic University

In 1971 Frances Fox Piven and Richard A. Cloward published their stimulating and provocative book, *Regulating the Poor: The Functions of Public Welfare,* in which they argued that relief systems undergo cycles of expansion and contraction, depending on "the problems of regulation in the larger society with which government must contend." The public welfare system in the United States, they believe, has historically served as a mechanism of social control, alternately used to maintain civil order or to enforce work norms. According to Piven and Cloward, the cycle works in the following way: "First, when mass unemployment leads to outbreaks of turmoil, relief programs are ordinarily initiated or expanded to absorb and control enough of the unemployed to restore order; then, as turbulence subsides, the relief system contracts, expelling those who are needed to populate the labor market." Government welfare programs, Piven and Cloward contend, have simply served as an effective way of manipulating the poor, keeping them orderly and, when appropriate, forcing them into low-income and menial employment.[1]

Piven and Cloward support their argument with several historical examples. After a brief discussion of relief developments in France during the sixteenth century and in England from the sixteenth through the nineteenth centuries, they move on to two examples drawn from the United States in the twentieth century. During the 1930s and the 1960s, they contend, the cyclical pattern of public welfare prevailed. During the Great Depression, for instance, massive unemployment, demonstrations and violence by the jobless, and the threat of leftist politicians brought the implementation of New Deal relief policies—first direct relief and later work relief. As political and social disorder declined in the late 1930s, federal welfare was reduced and needy people were forced to depend on poorly funded state and local relief agencies or move back into the private job market. Similarly, during the 1960s, civil disorder, rioting, and violence in the black ghettos of urban America stimulated a tremendous expansion of the welfare rolls. But by the early 1970s, as social disorder and racial conflict subsided, federal and state governments tightened up the welfare system, cut relief appropriations, and implemented deterrents of various kinds—all designed, as Richard Nixon often asserted, to move the poor off the welfare rolls and on to payrolls.

These are very challenging views, especially to those who conceive of relief programs as altruistic and humanitarian efforts to assist those in need. I do not know enough about sixteenth-century France or medieval England to say whether Piven and Cloward are right or wrong for those times and places. They may be correct for the 1930s and 1960s, although their argument remains essentially unproved and seems overly contrived in places. The story for both decades is a lot more complicated than they make it appear to be. But the real problem with the Piven and Cloward thesis is that it is presented as a single, unchanging, mechanical model. Although the authors have not said so outright, they have implied that this model is applicable throughout history—at least from the middle ages to the present. By way of testing the applicability of the Piven and Cloward thesis, let us look at a period of widespread depression, unemployment, social disorder, and violence they did not examine: the late nineteenth century.

In the thirty years between 1870 and 1900, the United States experienced three periods of prolonged economic depression. The depression of 1873-78 brought the most serious economic downturn in American history to that time. The impact was most apparent in the industrial cities of the northeast and midwest. During the depression winter of 1873-74, for example, about 40,000 laborers in Philadelphia were thrown out of work, while in New York City, almost 100,000 workers—one-quarter of the labor force—went jobless. In November 1874, according to the American Iron and Steel Institute, the number of unemployed reached at least 1 million. By the winter of 1877-78, unemployment nationwide peaked at 3 million. Labor reformer William G. Moody estimated in 1878 that one-half of the nation's working population was either wholly or partially unemployed. These economic conditions brought serious social unrest, labor discontent, and political agitation. In many cities, jobless workers established "unemployed councils" and "breadwinners leagues." They organized mass marches and demonstrations and demanded work, relief, and economic reform. Occasionally, these mass meetings and demonstrations resulted in violence, such as the Tompkins Square Riot in New York in January 1874, in which ten to fifteen thousand labor demonstrators were attacked and dispersed by police. The depression also stimulated radical politics and radical labor unionism. The mid-seventies witnessed the emergence of the national Greenback-Labor Party, the Socialist Labor Party, the Knights of Labor, and other political and labor groups. Layoffs and wage reductions brought a rash of work stoppages and labor violence, culminating in the great railroad strikes of 1877. State militias and even federal troops were called out to put down the striking railroad workers, but at great cost in lives — fifty-five workers and soldiers were killed in Pittsburgh alone. Thus, the combination of depression, massive unemployment, labor discontent, and radical agitation produced unprecedented social turmoil and disorder during the 1870s.[2]

A similar story might be told for the depression of 1882-86. Although less severe than that of the previous decade, this downturn in the business cycle was clearly an industrial depression rather than a business or financial panic, and its chief characteristics were wage cuts, layoffs, and unemployment among urban and industrial workers. By October 1884, according to one contemporary survey, unemployment reached 350,000 in twenty-two northern states, or about 13 percent of the work force, while wage cuts averaging 20 to 30 percent prevailed for those still working. The Massachusetts Bureau of Labor Statistics reported that in 1884-85 some 241,000 workers, or about 30 percent of the state's labor force, had been without jobs for an average of four months during the year. Employment statistics in Illinois revealed a similar picture, with 85,000 industrial workers laboring an average of thirty-seven weeks per year during 1885-86. By 1885, the newly created U.S. Bureau of Labor reported 1 million workers unemployed, while Terrence Powderly of the Knights of Labor insisted that the depression had idled at least 2 million. Unemployment and wage cuts intensified discontent and unrest among the working classes and stimulated new strike activity; some 8,584 recorded strike actions took place during the 1880s, including the notorious Haymarket Riot in Chicago in 1886, which touched off renewed fears of radicalism and violence from below.[3]

The nineteenth century ended with yet another period of depression. Like its predecessors, the depression of 1893–97 brought bank and business failures, wage cuts for some workers and unemployment for many others, mass demonstrations by the jobless, social and political radicalism, strikes, and violence. An economist at the University of Chicago surveyed unemployment in sixty cities in November 1893 and reported 100,000 out of work in Chicago; 85,000 in New York City; 50,000 in Philadelphia; 38,000 in Boston; 35,000 in Brooklyn; 25,000 in Detroit; 20,000 in St. Louis; 18,000 in Milwaukee; 15,000 in Cleveland, Buffalo, and Newark; and 10,000 in Baltimore, Providence, Paterson, and Rochester. Estimates of aggregate unemployment during the devastating winter of 1893–94 ranged from 1 to 4.5 million. While these statistics remain unproved, especially the larger figures offered by labor spokesmen, they suggest the relative magnitude of the depression of the nineties. Unemployed workers tramped the country in search of work; they demanded public jobs, food, and relief; they organized mass meetings and demonstrations; they went on strike to oppose wage cuts and layoffs. Many supported political change through populism, socialism, and other radical or utopian schemes. Led by Jacob Coxey and others, thousands of men demanding work and relief formed "industrial armies" and marched on Washington, a technique that has become increasingly popular in the twentieth century. The depression of 1893 was also marked by the most serious industrial conflict of the late nineteenth century—the Pullman Strike—which pitted federal troops against striking railroad workers, left dozens dead and wounded, and generated widespread fears of class conflict and revolution. According to the U.S. Bureau of Labor Statistics, more than 14,000 strikes involving about 3.7 million workers occurred during the 1890s.[4]

If space permitted, this tale of woe could be elaborated at length. Suffice it to say that these three depressions of the late nineteenth century should provide a clear test of the validity of the Piven and Cloward thesis. All of the requisite conditions prevailed during this period—massive unemployment, widespread discontent among the working class and the poor, the threat of political radicalism, mass marches, demonstrations, social disorder, and violence. If the Piven and Cloward model is correct, we should be able to find clear evidence of substantial expansion of public relief to temper the disorder among the unemployed and the poor, and then an effort to reinforce work norms when economic conditions improved and social turmoil subsided. Let us see what actually happened.

The late nineteenth century was crucial in the history of American social welfare. During this period, social welfare and philanthropy became rationalized, specialized, and "scientific." State boards of charities emerged in most states whose major function was to supervise administration of the various specialized state public welfare institutions, which included facilities for the blind, mentally ill, physically handicapped, medically indigent, and juvenile delinquent, as well as almshouses for the poor. The charity organization movement — an effort to systematize and coordinate private relief-giving at the local level — also sprouted during the last decades of the century. Toward the end of the period, settlement houses were established in cities to serve the immigrant and urban poor. These developments in public welfare and private charity stimulated the growth of professionalism in social work and social welfare.[5]

Simultaneously, a great debate raged about the relative merits of indoor versus outdoor relief. Public attitudes toward the poor were often uncharitable, to say the least. Most nineteenth-century Americans accepted the distinctions often drawn between the so-called worthy or deserving poor and those who were considered unworthy and thus undeserving. The American gospel of individualism continued to foster the belief that any hard-working, virtuous man could support his family in independence and dignity. Those in need, it was generally believed, had come to their dependent state through personal failings, such as immorality, idleness, intemperance, improvidence, and so on. Moreover, many agreed with industrialist Andrew Carnegie that poverty was a positive, character-building virtue, and that those with initiative and foresight would overcome their humble beginnings — the "rags to riches" theme of the Horatio Alger novels. Similarly, the social Darwinism of the time promoted acceptance of poverty and economic inequity as part of the natural order of things and cast further doubt on the usefulness of public relief and private charity. Adherents of this "survival of the fittest" theory of social relations believed, as one writer in *The Nation* put it in 1894, that the solution to poverty could be found in "nature's remedy" — "work or starve."[6]

The depressions of the late nineteenth century, then, occurred dur-

ing a significant period in American social welfare thought and practice. The response to the depressions varied from state to state and
from city to city. In some places, public assistance predominated,
in some places public funds were supplied to private charitable agencies, and in some places private charity took over fund-raising and
relief-giving entirely. Yet, despite the variety of charitable and relief
arrangements, three persistent patterns stand out clearly. First, from
the 1870s on a strong trend against public assistance prevailed, a trend
most observable in the complete abolition of outdoor relief in a number of major cities. Second, the state boards of charities in virtually
every state emphasized the need for charity "reform," — stressing that
charitable assistance should be economically, efficiently, and spar-
ingly distributed. Third, with the exception of some religious charities,
private philanthropy was virtually taken over by the charity organization societies (cos). The cos approach emphasized case-by-case
investigation to distinguish the worthy from the unworthy poor, advocated the careful distribution of aid to prevent duplication and
"impositions," and demanded the "work test" both as a deterrent
to relief-seekers and as a means to build character and self-respect
among recipients. These three developments — the abolition of outdoor relief in many cities, the emergence of the state charity boards,
and the rise of the cos movement — dictated and determined the
American response to unemployment and poverty during the three
depressions of the late nineteenth century.

The trend toward the abolition of outdoor relief became apparent
during the mid-1870s. To be sure, there had been a temporary increase in public assistance in many places, especially during the first
harsh depression winter of 1873–74, but the funds dispersed were
hardly magnanimous anywhere. Private charities rather than public
agencies shouldered most of the relief burden during the depression
of the seventies, as soup houses, free lodging houses, medical dispen-
saries, and the like were established. Even public work relief was
rejected by most municipalities. A movement by the unemployed
for public works developed in New York, Philadelphia, Cincinnati,
Detroit, Pittsburgh, Louisville, and other cities. However, despite
the obvious need and the potential violence threatened by mobs of
unemployed roaming the streets and demanding work, the movement for public works failed almost everywhere. One exception was
Boston, where the overseers of the poor hired jobless men for temporary work on street construction, but only three hundred men per

day were employed in this way. Boston, though, was not typical and, as one social welfare historian has noted, remained the only major eastern city to hold out against the movement to abolish outdoor relief.[7]

Indeed, the most significant development in public welfare during the period lay in the abandonment of outdoor relief by most of the nation's largest cities. In New York City, for instance, public outdoor relief was suspended in 1874 and, except for small appropriations for the indigent blind, was not resumed during the remainder of the nineteenth century. The 1898 charter of the newly consolidated Greater New York actually prohibited the distribution of outdoor relief. In Brooklyn, the nation's third-largest city, outdoor relief was abandoned in 1878. The relief system, Brooklyn's mayor Seth Low reported, had become "a sore on the body politic" and "a vast political corruption fraud." Low later contended that the move had placed no additional burdens on the almshouse or private charities, pointedly suggesting that outdoor relief supported worthless idlers and represented an expensive and useless drain on municipal treasuries. The trend continued the following year, as Philadelphia abolished outdoor relief in 1879. The results, Seth Low argued in a paper before the National Conference of Charities and Correction, were the same: no increase in pauperism and a reduced call on private charities. In both cities, he wrote, "private benevolence is equal to the burden of such outdoor relief as may be actually needed."[8]

In the 1870s, several other cities severely limited outdoor relief to those who performed some sort of work. Providence, Rhode Island, for example, spent more than $150,000 on outdoor relief in 1878; with the application of the "work test," the annual cost allegedly was reduced to $4,700 in 1880. In Cleveland, city officials claimed that the work requirement cut a $95,000 annual relief expense to $17,000 in 1880. Still other big cities, such as Chicago and Washington, appropriated virtually no public relief funds, leaving the outdoor poor to private charities. In Chicago, with the city treasury exhausted, the Chicago Relief and Aid Society simply took over the responsibility for outdoor relief and distributed surplus funds collected for victims of the great Chicago fire of 1871. In the nation's capital, outdoor relief was administered by the police department, but almost all of the money was raised by charities and private donations.[9]

The trend toward abolition of outdoor relief continued during the next two decades. No great expansion in public assistance occurred during the depressions of the 1880s and 1890s. Some cities experimented with work relief. Typically, Pittsburgh employed several thousand jobless men in a huge park-construction project, while Boston required relievers to cut wood for two days in return for two dollars worth of groceries. Most of the relief-giving during the depression of the nineties was done not by municipal governments or public agencies but by emergency citizens' committees, religious charities, newspaper relief funds, labor unions, and other voluntary societies. Meanwhile, additional cities were terminating public assistance. By 1900 outdoor relief had been abandoned in Baltimore, St. Louis, Washington, San Francisco, Kansas City, New Orleans, Louisville, Denver, Atlanta, Memphis, and Charleston. Several other large cities — Cincinnati, Jersey City, Indianapolis, Pittsburgh, Providence, and St. Paul — budgeted only miniscule amounts for outdoor relief compared to their total populations. According to a survey made in 1900, "of the 21 cities in this country having a population over 200,000, 10 give practically no public out-relief, and 2 more . . . give very little." The depressions of the late nineteenth century, rather than loosening public purse strings for the unemployed and the poor, hardened antipauperism attitudes and cast those in need onto private charity rolls.[10]

Thus, the Piven and Cloward model does not seem to fit the actual circumstances of public welfare in late-nineteenth-century America. Although responses to the depressions differed according to local conditions and local traditions, clearly there was no massive increase in public assistance to quiet the poor and the unemployed and to keep them orderly. The outbreaks of violence and rioting during strikes and demonstrations were not followed by increased relief to prevent further disorders. Rather, the ultimate social control — officially sanctioned violence by police and soldiers — was used against strikers, marchers, and demonstrators. And, of course, the abolition of outdoor relief in most of the nation's largest cities during the depression years is the exact opposite of what we might have expected to happen under the Piven and Cloward model.

Although the Piven and Cloward thesis seems incorrect when applied to the circumstances of the late nineteenth century, this does not mean that social welfare was not used for the purpose of social control. It only means that the social control mechanisms utilized in the Gilded Age were different from those identified by Piven and

Cloward. Both the charity organization movement and the new state boards of charities supply keys to understanding the ways in which charity and social welfare were used to control and manipulate the poor and to shape their behavior and their values.

The charity organization movement had a great impact in shaping social welfare thought and practice in the late nineteenth century. The cos movement officially began in 1877, when the Buffalo cos was founded. The new "scientific" philanthropy spread rapidly throughout urban America. At least twenty-five cities had established charity organization societies by 1883, and about one hundred had done so by 1895. Underpinning the entire cos movement were two fundamental beliefs: first, that poverty and dependency resulted from individual moral and character defects; and, second, that indiscriminate charity and public relief merely strengthened pauperism by discouraging the poor from making any efforts in their own behalf. This analysis of the problem dictated the cos solutions: that urban charity should be rationalized and coordinated to eliminate duplication of effort; that relief applicants should be carefully investigated before being granted any aid; that relief should be minimal and temporary and if possible tied to work; and that the morals and the behavior of the poor should be regulated and reformed. In the words of one social welfare historian, the cos "emphasized personal failure as the major cause of dependency, believed that no one would work unless goaded by fear of starvation, investigated every aspect of an applicant's life, reduced relief to the lowest possible level, and provided close supervision of any family on its rolls."[11]

Most recent historians of the cos movement have agreed on the social control purposes of the "new charity." cos philanthropy was built upon the work of the "friendly visitors" — middle-class female volunteers who went into the slums to counsel the poor and guide them onto the paths of work and virtue. These cos workers hoped to end pauperism and associated social evils by cultivating such decent and proper middle-class values as thrift, honesty, work, self-reliance, sobriety, piety, respect for authority, and the like. Moral uplift and character building through friendly visiting represented nothing less than the shaping and regulating of behavior. cos advocates optimistically contended that this sort of moralistic paternalism — or maternalism — would not only improve the lot of the poor but also restore social unity, strengthen family ties, protect wealth and property, counter socialist and radical schemes, and safeguard against revolution from below.[12]

If the COS demanded virtue from the poor, they also vigorously promoted the work ethic and urged various deterrents to charity and relief. COS leaders castigated public assistance and in many cities led the successful drive against public outdoor relief. Josephine Shaw Lowell, a founder of the New York COS and a vigorous propagandist for the entire movement, argued that any sort of relief "should be surrounded by circumstances that shall . . . repel every one, not in extremity, from accepting it." Relief was a last resort for the helpless poor, she believed, and even then the COS should "refuse to support any except those whom it can control." Even work relief, Lowell contended, was "dangerous"; to effectively counter pauperism and dependency, work relief had to be "continuous, hard, and underpaid." In an 1894 article in *The Nation,* another COS advocate was equally blunt about those who refused to work and earn "an honest living": "The time has come to cross-examine the unemployed, to ask them how they came into their present evil estate, what work they ever did and how they came to lose their jobs, and what work they could or would do now if it were offered them." The real solution to poverty, this uncharitable COS analyst asserted, was not to provide work relief, since that only interfered with natural economic laws, "but to make men competent and willing to work." "The great lesson we want to teach people," Josephine Shaw Lowell wrote, "is to depend on themselves." Clearly, the COS movement promoted work and self-reliance in answer to the economic dislocations of the late nineteenth century.[13]

Closely related to the COS movement were the state charity boards that emerged about the same time. Established in most states prior to 1900, the new boards of charities offered similar analyses of the problems of dependency and public assistance. Not surprisingly, many COS people were involved with the state charity boards. Josephine Shaw Lowell, for instance, one of the founders of the New York COS, was a long-term member of the New York State Board of Charities and a member of its standing committee on outdoor relief. Like the COS, the state boards pursued the ideals of scientific charity and sought to shape the values and to control the behavior of the poor.

The state charity boards were charged primarily with administering various state welfare institutions in more rational and efficient ways. But they also investigated all aspects of relief-giving, collected reams of statistics, and delivered annual analyses of the poverty problem. Uniformly, the state charity boards condemned outdoor relief. As early as 1875, a report of the New York State Board of Charities recommended against outdoor relief. "The wisest and safest course," the report suggested, "would be ultimately to abolish all official outdoor relief, to improve and enlarge the accommodation in the institutions, and to throw the responsibility of providing for the wants of the worthy poor entirely on existing private charitable agencies." In 1879, the New York board declared that outdoor relief was "injurious and hurtful to the unfortunate and worthy poor, demoralizing in its tendencies, a prolific source of pauperism and official corruption, and an unjust burden upon the public." Similarly, in 1884 the board argued that outdoor relief was "not only useless, as a means to relieving actual existing suffering, but an active means of increasing present and future want and vice." The administration of outdoor relief remained a matter of local control in New York, but the state board of charities took a firm and consistent stand against this form of public welfare throughout the period.[14]

The story was the same in Ohio. Reporting in 1884, the Ohio Board of State Charities asserted outdoor relief to be "a dangerous expenditure, as it tends rapidly to undermine habits of industry, economy, and self-reliance, and to pauperize whole families." What was to be done? The Ohio board had a suggestion: "We believe it would be wise to put a stop to all outdoor relief in cities, leaving the care of those needing aid to private charities. This experiment has been tried in the cities of Buffalo, Brooklyn, Philadelphia, Indianapolis, and other places, with entire success, and is found to furnish more ample relief to the deserving poor, while it saves a large amount to the tax-payers." The Ohio charities board held to this view through the end of the nineteenth century, repeatedly advocating the abolition of outdoor relief. The outdoor relief system, social gospeler Washington Gladden noted in an 1891 address to the annual Ohio Conference on Charities, encouraged pauperism, undermined self-reliance and industry, and corrupted the political process. Outdoor relief, Gladden contended, was "a cancer . . . eating out the heart of our social morality."[15]

Similar arguments against outdoor relief were advocated by charity boards in other states as well. In 1873, for example, the Rhode Island Board of State Charities and Corrections condemned outdoor relief because it "does more hurt than good, and makes more paupers than it relieves."[16] Outdoor relief, wrote Washington, D.C., superintendent of charities Amos Warner in 1892, "is one of the most dangerous methods of relieving the poor ever attempted."[17] In Pennsylvania, the Board of Commissioners of Public Charities held similar views. "Large numbers of persons naturally idle and improvident," the board reported in 1880, "have been trained and educated for the poor house by outdoor relief carelessly and prodigally administered."[18] Outdoor relief came under scathing attack virtually everywhere in the last three decades of the nineteenth century.

Like the cos, state charity officials sought not only to terminate outdoor relief but also to build character, morality, and self-reliance among the poor. Since most pauperism stemmed from intemperance, the Pennsylvania state charity commissioners asserted in 1871, the evils of relief could be avoided if "the victims of appetite, and lust, and idleness" were trained "to know and revere the precepts of the Bible, and to form habits of industry, frugality, and self-restraint."[19] The outdoor poor, the Minnesota State Board of Corrections and Charities suggested in 1896, could best be aided "by cultivating habits of independence and thrift."[20] Reporting in 1890, the Ohio Board of State Charities noted that "the most practical, helpful and useful form of charity, whether considered from its effects upon the community or the individual, is to encourage everybody, as far as possible, to provide for themselves."[21] For public charity officers in Massachusetts in 1900, the answer to the outdoor relief problem was clear and simple; the only way of "meeting the evil of idleness" was through "the provision of work."[22] Relief officials in Indiana held to a similar position: "Nothing creates pauperism so rapidly as the giving of relief to persons without requiring them to earn what they receive by some kind of honest labor."[23]

Thus, the state boards of charities provided a second important force for regulating the poor. They sought to bring the principles of efficiency, economy, and rationality to public welfare agencies and institutions. By systematically gathering information and statistics about poverty, public health, crime, and other social conditions, they initiated the development of a professional social science.[24] Their investigations led them to condemn outdoor relief and even demand its total abolition. Like the cos, the state charity boards urged careful investigation of relief applicants to separate the worthy from the unworthy poor. They believed that private charity could provide for all those who truly needed temporary assistance or those who did not require institutionalization. Finally, they sought to make the poor industrious, religious, temperate, thrifty, and self-reliant. Above all, it was believed that if the poor worked hard they would not become dependent. This emphasis on character building clearly marks the state charity boards as agencies seeking to control the poor.

In conclusion, then, the Piven and Cloward model of regulating the poor does not conform to the reality of American social welfare history in the late nineteenth century. Despite widespread unemployment, poverty, social turmoil, and violence, public relief was not expanded to help the poor or to calm social disorder. Rather, city after city abandoned public outdoor relief in accordance with the new scientific philanthropy of the period. Mass demonstrations, disorder, and violence were dealt with through such traditional social controls as law, penal institutions, police, militia, even federal troops. However, social welfare was used for social control purposes, not in the ways suggested by Piven and Cloward, but through the charity organization societies and the state boards of charities, which vigorously sought to regulate and shape the values and behavior of the poor. Piven and Cloward deserve a great deal of credit for forcefully raising questions about who benefits and whose interests are protected or advanced by social welfare policies and programs.[25] This analysis of social welfare in late-nineteenth-century America, however, demonstrates the inadequacy of a single, unchanging, inflexible historical interpretation of human behavior. In the context of the social welfare history of the late nineteenth century, the Piven and Cloward thesis seems untenable.

NOTES

1. Frances Fox Piven and Richard A. Cloward, *Regulating the Poor: The Functions of Public Welfare* (New York: Pantheon, 1971), xiii, 3. The thesis is summarized in Frances Fox Piven and Richard A. Cloward, "The Relief of Welfare," *Trans-action* 8 (May 1971), 31–39, 52–53, and Frances Fox Piven and Richard A. Cloward, "How the Federal Government Caused the Welfare Crisis," *Social Policy* 2 (May–June 1971), 40–49.

2. Samuel Rezneck, "Distress, Relief and Discontent in the United States during the Depression of 1873–78," *Journal of Political Economy* 58 (Dec. 1950), 494–512; Philip S. Foner, *History of the Labor Movement in the United*

States, 4 vols. (New York: International Publishers, 1947-67), 1:439-96; Leah Hannah Feder, *Unemployment Relief in Periods of Depression* (New York: Russell Sage, 1936), 37-43; Robert L. Heilbroner, *The Economic Transformation of America* (New York: Harcourt Brace Jovanovich, 1977), 106, 133; Herbert G. Gutman, "The Failure of the Movement by the Unemployed for Public Works in 1873," *Political Science Quarterly* 80 (June 1965), 254-76, and "The Tompkins Square 'Riot' in New York City on January 13, 1874: A Re-examination of Its Causes and Its Aftermath," *Labor History,* 6 (Winter 1965), 44-70; Robert V. Bruce, *1877: Year of Violence* (Indianapolis: Bobbs-Merrill, 1959); Jerry M. Cooper, *The Army and Civil Disorder: Federal Military Intervention in Labor Disputes, 1877-1900* (Westport, Conn.: Greenwood, 1980).

3. Samuel Rezneck, "Patterns of Thought and Action in an American Depression, 1882-1886," *American Historical Review* 61 (Jan. 1956), 284-306; Henry David, *The History of the Haymarket Affair* (New York: Farrarr and Rinehart, 1936), 20; Harold G. Vatter, *The Drive to Industrial Maturity: The U.S. Economy, 1860-1914* (Westport, Conn.: Greenwood, 1975), 280-97; Florence Peterson, *Strikes in the United States, 1880-1936* (U.S. Department of Labor, Bulletin No. 651; Washington, D.C.: G. P. O., 1938), 27, 29.

4. Carlos C. Clossen, Jr., "The Unemployed in American Cities," *Quarterly Journal of Economics* 8 (Jan. 1894), 257-59; Samuel Rezneck, "Unemployment, Unrest, and Relief in the United States during the Depression of 1893-97," *Journal of Political Economy* 61 (Aug. 1953), 324-45; Douglas W. Steeples, "The Panic of 1893: Contemporary Reflections and Reactions," *Mid-America* 47 (July 1965), 155-75; Charles Hoffman, *The Depression of the Nineties: An Economic History* (Westport, Conn.: Greenwood, 1970), 47-112; Paul T. Ringenbach, *Tramps and Reformers, 1873-1916: The Discovery of Unemployment in New York* (Westport, Conn.: Greenwood, 1973), 36-81; Feder, *Unemployment Relief,* 76-85; Foner, *History of the Labor Movement in the United States,* 2: 235-46, 261-78; Peterson, *Strikes in the United States,* 29.

5. On social welfare developments in the late nineteenth century, see Robert H. Bremner, *From the Depths: The Discovery of Poverty in the United States* (New York: New York Univ. Press, 1956), 16-85; Robert H. Bremner, "Scientific Philanthropy, 1873-1893," *Social Service Review* 30 (June 1956), 168-73; Frank J. Bruno, *Trends in Social Work, 1874-1956* (New York: Columbia Univ. Press, 1957), 25-43, 96-118; Hace Sorel Tishler, *Self-Reliance and Social Security, 1870-1917* (Port Washington, N.Y.: Kennikat, 1971), 3-79; Walter I. Trattner, *From Poor Law to Welfare State: A History of Social Welfare in America* (New York: Free Press, 1974), 75-95; James Leiby, *A History of Social Welfare and Social Work in the United States* (New York: Columbia Univ. Press, 1978), 71-135; Blanche D. Coll, *Perspectives in Public Welfare: A History* (Washington, D.C.: G. P. O., 1969).

6. Rollo Ogden, "The Real Problem of the Unemployed," *The Nation* 59 (5 July 1894), 6.

7. Feder, *Unemployment Relief,* 44-70; Gutman, "The Failure of the Movement by the Unemployed for Public Works in 1873," 254-76; Samuel

Mencher, *Poor Law to Poverty Program: Economic Security Policy in Britain and the United States* (Pittsburgh: Univ. of Pittsburgh Press, 1967), 282. For a study of social welfare thought and practice in Boston during this period, see Nathan Irvin Huggins, *Protestants Against Poverty: Boston's Charities, 1870–1900* (Westport, Conn.: Greenwood, 1971). Typical contemporary articles reflecting opposition to outdoor relief in the 1870s include Robert T. Davis, "Pauperism in the City of New York," *Journal of Social Science* 6 (July 1874), 74–83; H.L. Wayland, "Report on Out-Door Relief," *Proceedings of the Eighth Annual Conference of Charities* [hereafter cited as *ACC*], *1877* (Boston, George H. Ellis, 1877), 46–59.

8. Feder, *Unemployment Relief*, 49: Barry J. Kaplan, "Reformers and Charity: The Abolition of Public Outdoor Relief in New York City, 1870–1898," *Social Science Review* 52 (June 1978), 202–14; Seth Low, "The Problem of Pauperism in the Cities of Brooklyn and New York," *ACC, 1879* (Boston: George H. Ellis, 1879), 200–210; Seth Low, "Out-Door Relief in the United States," *ACC, 1881* (Boston: George H. Ellis, 1881), 144–54.

9. Low, "Out-Door Relief in the United States," 152; *The Sixteenth Annual Report of the Chicago Relief and Aid Society* (Chicago: Relief and Aid Society, 1874), 6; Otto M. Nelson, "The Chicago Relief and Aid Society, 1850–1874," *Illinois State Historical Society Journal* 59 (Spring 1966), 48–66; Timothy J. Naylor, "Responding to the Fire: The Work of the Chicago Relief and Aid Society," *Science and Society* 39 (Winter 1975–76), 450–64; Edward T. Devine, "Public Outdoor Relief," *Charities Review* 8 (June 1898), 188–89.

10. Albert Shaw, "Relief for the Unemployed in American Cities," *Review of Reviews* 9 (Jan. 1894), 36–37; Closson, "The Unemployed in American Cities," 181; Feder, *Unemployment Relief,* 170; Homer Folks, "Report of the Committee on Municipal and County Charities," *Proceedings of the National Conference of Charities and Correction* [hereafter cited as *NCCC*], *1898* (Boston: George H. Ellis, 1899), 106–83; Homer Folks, "Municipal Charities," *Municipal Affairs* 3 (Sept. 1899), 516–27; Frederic Almy, "Public or Private Outdoor Relief," *NCCC, 1900* (Boston: George H. Ellis, 1901), 134–45, quotation on p. 138.

11. Frank Dekker, Watson, *The Charity Organization Movement in the United States* (New York: Macmillan, 1922), 179–86, 222; Coll, *Perspectives in Public Welfare,* 62.

12. The social control functions of the cos movement are emphasized in Roy Lubove, *The Professional Altruist: The Emergence of Social Work as a Career, 1880–1930* (Cambridge, Mass.: Harvard Univ. Press, 1965), 1–21; Paul Boyer, *Urban Masses and Moral Order in America, 1820–1920* (Cambridge, Mass.: Harvard Univ. Press, 1978), 143–61; Marvin E. Gettleman, "Charity and Social Classes in the United States, 1874–1900," *American Journal of Economics and Sociology* 22 (April 1963), 313–29, (July 1963), 417–26; Marvin E. Gettleman, "Philanthropy as Social Control in Late Nineteenth-Century America: Some Hypotheses and Data on the Rise of Social Work," *Societas—a Review of Social History,* 5 (Winter 1975), 49–59.

13. Josephine Shaw Lowell, *Public Relief and Private Charity* (New York: N.Y. Charity Organ. Society, 1884), 67–68, and "Methods of Relief for the

Unemployed," *The Forum* 16 (Feb. 1894), 660; Ogden, "The Real Problem of the Unemployed," 6; William Rhinelander Stewart, ed., *The Philanthropic Work of Josephine Shaw Lowell* (New York: Macmillan, 1911), 147; Piven and Cloward, *Regulating the Poor,* 97.

14. State of New York, *Ninth Annual Report of the State Board of Charities* (Albany, 1876), 133; *Twelfth Annual Report of the State Board of Charities* (Albany, 1879), 30; and *Seventeenth Annual Report of the State Board of Charities* (Albany, 1884), 160.

15. State of Ohio, *Ninth Annual Report of the Board of State Charities* (Columbus, 1885), 8–9; *Sixteenth Annual Report of the Board of State Charities* (Columbus, 1892), 314–16.

16. State of Rhode Island, *Fifth Annual Report of the Board of State Charities and Corrections of Rhode Island, 1873* (Providence, 1874), 62.

17. *Report of the Superintendent of Charities for the District of Columbia for the Year Ending June 30, 1892* (Washington, D.C., 1892), 48.

18. *Eleventh Annual Report of the Board of Commissioners of Public Charities of the State of Pennsylvania* (Harrisburg, 1881), 5.

19. *First Annual Report of the Board of Commissioners of Public Charities of the State of Pennsylvania* (Harrisburg, 1871), liii.

20. *Minnesota Bulletin of Charities and Correction* 10 (Dec. 1896), 52.

21. State of Ohio, *Fifteenth Annual Report of the Board of State Charities* (Columbus, 1891), 30.

22. Massachusetts Association of Relief Officers, *Report on the Best Methods of Dealing with Tramps and Wayfarers* (Boston, 1901), 8.

23. *Indiana Bulletin of Charities and Correction* (December 1895), 8.

24. Thomas L. Haskell, *The Emergence of Professional Social Science: The American Social Science Association and the Nineteenth-Century Crisis of Authority* (Urbana: Univ. of Illinois Press, 1977), 91–97.

25. On these points, see Marvin E. Gettleman, "The Whig Interpretation of Social Welfare History," *Smith College Studies in Social Work* 44 (June 1974), 149–57, and Raymond A. Mohl, "Mainstream Social Welfare History and Its Problems," *Reviews in American History* 7 (Dec. 1979), 469–76.

THE WIDOWS' PENSION MOVEMENT, 1900–1930:

Preventive Child-Saving or Social Control?

MURIEL W. PUMPHREY
University of Missouri–St. Louis

and

RALPH E. PUMPHREY
Washington University in St. Louis

In the decade preceding World War I traditional social structures were under scrutiny and reform movements "caught on" in various segments of the population; some even made their way into law and administrative practice. One such development was the idea that government should provide financial help to widows (and possibly other mothers) faced with the burden of raising their families without the support of male breadwinners. Widows', or mothers', pension laws, as they were called, were passed in many states beginning in 1911. These became precursors to both the Aid to Families with Dependent Children (AFDC) and the Survivors Insurance programs under the Social Security Act.

During the seventy years or so since their enactment, various shortcomings in these programs have concerned social workers and taxpayers as well as administrators and politicians, not to mention the recipients of the often inadequate financial aid. Frances Piven and Richard Cloward have been among the most severe such critics. Revolted, among other things, by the AFDC program of the 1960s, they put their concerns in a broader context in their highly acclaimed work, *Regulating the Poor*. In it, they said that AFDC and other assistance programs were devised to forestall disturbances among unemployed and poorly paid workers during times of economic distress and to maintain a large supply of low-paid workers in times of prosperity.[1]

This is a dramatic proposition, one that contrasts sharply with traditional interpretations of American social welfare history. Unfortunately, however, it is supported, insofar as widows' pensions are concerned, only by secondary reports of legislative and administrative outcomes. By implication, these outcomes become identified with the intent of the advocates, although no evidence is supplied to support the connection.[2]

Sound historical analysis would have required that the stated intent of the proponents of the measures be examined in relation to the conditions to be changed, and that the outcome be judged as much by what was accomplished as by what was not. Instead, the authors gratuitously attribute to the widows' aid movement of two generations ago the same evil intent they claim to observe in today's AFDC program. Given the scantiness of the evidence they adduce, largely circumstantial in nature, this aspect of their argument would hardly stand in a court of law.

Rather than attempt to prove or disprove such innuendos, we have chosen to examine the widows' pension movement from a standpoint Piven and Cloward chose not to consider—the process by which the new idea was incorporated into, and reached an accommodation with, the older cultural and legal system.

The initial thrust of the widows' pension movement was to secure adequate, regular, assured assistance for mothers who otherwise would have been forced into what we now call "the secondary labor market" to the detriment of their own health and to the neglect and demoralization of their children. That the movement's proponents sought to change existing social controls is undeniable. That accomplishments fell far short of rhetoric also is undeniable. That the objective was to "grind the faces of the poor," to use the biblical phrase, by assuring a supply of surplus labor and by propping up a system of inadequate wages is not at all evident. Indeed, just the opposite seems to be true.

The struggle for widows' pensions can be seen as a contest between two concepts of social control. The first was represented by traditional laissez-faire self-help and the second by the emerging concept of preventive child-saving which sought to eliminate child labor and child prostitution, improve nutrition and educational opportunities, and preserve families intact. Major components of the traditional point of view were parochialism and a general rejection of superior authority and supervision both by governments and by care-taking institutions. The new view emphasized breadth of vision and the responsibility and capacity of government to deal with problems.

Caught between these were the roles and integrity of municipal governments, private agencies, and individual functionaries.

The optimistic literary version of laissez-faire was well represented in the Horatio Alger novels and the volumes of biographical sketches by Samuel Smiles. Negative reality was found everywhere in the centuries-old English and American Poor Law, clothed in its refined doctrine of "lesser eligibility." Help from the public treasury was to be so given "that, presumably, persons not in danger of starvation will not consent to receive it."[3]

The Poor Law was but one aspect of the interrelationship of government with capitalism, both agrarian and industrial. Low wages, job insecurity, uncompensated work accidents, and illness all left families vulnerable to destitution when the wage-earner was disabled or dead. Since the responsibility of a widow to care for herself and her family was unquestioned, the responsibility of the state began only after she had failed. This meant that in addition to her socially and economically valuable homemaking responsibilities, she must undertake to replace the earnings of her deceased husband. If she did not earn enough, and few could, she might enlist the help of her children in eking out a bare existence until illness or the neglect or delinquency of the youngsters forced her to surrender them for placement in an institution or foster home, often with no residual rights, even to visit them.[4]

The "rightness" of such arrangements is illustrated by the response of an institution superintendent to a Massachusetts questionnaire in 1912: "To me," he stated, "it seems very natural that our institution should take children from widows for 'poverty alone,' since the care of the children by the mother would hinder her from going out to earn money. And if she were to go out . . . the children would certainly not grow up to what they ought to be."[5]

The literature of the charity organization societies (cos), which had helped to do away with public outdoor relief in many cities, was full of similar assertions: "Any able bodied woman of average natural ability can manage to support herself and her children if there is enough insurance to provide for the necessities of the family for a few weeks."[6] Or, in the words of yet another supporter of the traditional approach, "A widow may desire to . . . work for [her children's] support, and yet be hindered from securing employment so long as she must keep them together in a home. Temporary care . . . may be the wisest and most humane method."[7]

As a result of these attitudes and policies, an ever increasing number of dependent and neglected children were being cared for in institutions. The highest rate appears to have come in about 1910, when it is estimated that more than 126,000, or more than three per thousand of the child population, were institutionalized.[8] This was only a part of the family disruption going on at that time, for over 17,000 destitute children were "placed out" in foster homes by institutions and agencies during the year 1907 alone.[9]

In opposition to the economic, legal, and institutional establishments was a varied group of reformers developing different strategies. At first, widows' pensions were not one of their major interests. Massachusetts, Michigan, and Minnesota had early developed foster home programs to remove children from almshouses and to avoid stultifying institutional life, but few states had followed suit. Everywhere, routine removal of children from their homes had come under sharp attack. Delinquency and the handling of children in courts and correctional systems had led to the establishment of juvenile courts. The hazards to children in industry and their lack of schooling had sparked drives for child-labor and compulsory education laws. Groups working for a "living" wage and social insurance added to the clamor by urging that children should be protected from malnutrition and poor living conditions due to preventable hazards. Until those distant goals could be reached they also urged immediate adequate provision for destitute families.[10]

As the first decade of the twentieth century progressed, these different movements turned out to have one thing in common: concern over unnecessary, expensive, and socially destructive breaking up of homes. Those opposed to large institutions subsidized by New York and other states claimed that with the same money given promptly, mothers could provide adequate homes without long hours of drudgery resulting in family neglect. Traditionally, child labor was thought to be essential in families where the mother's earnings were insufficient, but working children could attend school irregularly at best. Both opponents of child labor and proponents of compulsory education therefore favored measures to support mothers in their homes. In addition, settlement house residents provided early, vocal, and consistent advocacy for many aspects of child-saving, including this one.[11]

The year 1909 saw these and other forces converge dramatically at the first White House Conference on the Care of Dependent Children. The report issued by the conference, with the endorsement of President Theodore Roosevelt, proclaimed, "Home life is the highest and finest product of civilization. . . . Except in unusual circumstances, the home should not be broken up for reasons of poverty." That bold statement, however, included qualifying phrases reflecting the dominant ideas of the time — "parents of worthy character," "reasonably efficient and deserving mothers," "aid necessary to maintain suitable homes," "considerations of inefficiency and immorality," and "private charity rather than public relief."[12]

In spite of its seeming suddenness, widows' pension legislation, which followed the White House Conference by two years, did not break entirely new ground. As early as 1880 California had authorized state subsidies to local poor relief officials to help mothers keep their children at home.[13] The respected Franklin Sanborn of Massachusetts had advocated "family aid" at the National Conference of Charities and Correction in 1890, but his words were overwhelmed by the "lesser eligibility" eloquence of Josephine Shaw Lowell, the patrician leader of the New York cos.[14] In 1894 Amos Warner, himself a former official of both public and private charitable agencies, weighed Sanborn's and Lowell's arguments and concluded that it was the administration of relief that tipped the scales against public outdoor assistance: "It must be remembered," he declared, "that the people of the United States have a larger share of administrative awkwardness than any other civilized population."[15]

With the passage of time, however, the emphasis of cos rhetoric began to shift from a negative campaign against "pauperism" to an effort to rescue those who were on the brink of that condition. "Worthy" widows with children might be helped to maintain their homes by regular financial support — if funds were available. This modification of the self-help dogma came hard, but in 1898 an arrangement was worked out between the New York cos and the city Department of Public Charities under which the cos was allowed to visit families petitioning for commitment of children. If the cos decided the preservation of a specific family could be accomplished by a combination of casework services and specially mobilized financial aid, the Department would leave the case in the care of the cos. By 1901, the cos had accumulated a load of 350 cases, including 800 children who otherwise would have become public charges.[16] Thus, for some, the limited funds available had eased somewhat the implacable requirements of long, hard labor at starvation wages. To keep this in perspective, however, we should note that in 1900 alone the New York Society for the Prevention of Cruelty to Children placed 2,407 children in institutional care.[17]

If the New York experiment was limited in scope, many other local charity organization societies began to recognize that adequate relief, promptly and regularly given over extended periods of time, was effective in preventing family breakdown. However, the deep-seated suspicion and antipathy toward public administration, as well as a realistic perception of the probable inadequacies of public appropriations, kept most cos leaders at least on the sidelines, if not in opposition to mothers' pension proposals. Successful drives for the passage of such proposals came from other quarters, with the cos performing a braking function.[18]

Transitional thinking had been expressed in 1900 by the head of the Minnesota state child-placing agency: "Permanent separation of a child from its natural parents . . . should be permitted only when parents cannot be helped or compelled to meet their obligations. . . . Poverty alone is not always a sufficient cause for such action," he concluded.[19]

Meanwhile, various bodies, including the National Child Labor Committee and the National Consumers' League, were carrying on a militant campaign against child labor, including the idea of scholarship aid to help needy children stay in school. As a result, in 1908 the new state of Oklahoma included in its compulsory education law provision for allowances for needy mothers.[20]

Juvenile courts also became concentrated galleries for the display of the dismal effects on children of the prevailing disregard of the needs of poverty-stricken families.[21] Thus, in Chicago, shortly after the White House Conference, the judge of the juvenile court and his chief probation officer, the secretary of the National Probation League, began pressing for legislative authorization for court-mandated allowances to mothers of dependent children. Their success, in 1911, made Illinois the first state to provide statewide authorization for local bodies — juvenile courts — to administer pensions to mothers outside the established welfare system. Although only a few Illinois counties were quick to implement these provisions, leading Chicagoans became spokespersons for the new movement.[22]

Missouri, which had more children in private institutions than any state except New York and Massachusetts, came up with separate plans for its two major cities. Kansas City adopted a juvenile court plan providing pensions for widows. This was expanded in 1913 to include wives of men in prisons or insane asylums and was extended in 1917 to make it optional in all counties of the state. In St. Louis, all child welfare services, including an institution for delinquents as well as foster-home care for dependent and neglected children, were concentrated in a newly created Board of Childrens' Guardians. Perhaps following a pattern of Poor Law administration adopted in Indiana several years before, or a 1910 ruling in New Jersey, the members of this Board were given authority to "board" children in their own homes, with aid being given to the mother.[23]

Colorado, by popular vote in 1912, also adopted juvenile court administration.[24] By 1913, "the wave of mothers' pension agitation and legislation that was sweeping over the country"[25] led to a variety of measures. New Jersey formally enacted a widows' pension law.[26] California strengthened its long dormant aid-to-mothers programs by permitting counties to match state funds.[27] Pennsylvania, "caught in an irresistible tide of public sentiment," passed a measure under which administration was left to unguided, unsupervised local boards of women in those counties that chose to act. Deserted wives as well as widows were eligible. Although the appropriation was "ludicrously inadequate," some inducement was offered in the form of state matching funds. In 1915 provision for deserted wives was eliminated and a supervisory office was established in the State Board of Education.[28]

Again in 1913, Massachusetts revised its relatively liberal Poor Law to make the State Board of Charity responsible for supervising the work of local overseers of the poor with respect to all cases in which there were one or more children under the age of fourteen. This infringement on the traditional autonomy of the overseers, however, was not done for punitive purposes; the Massachusetts authorities insisted that the statute was "an *adequate relief* measure, not a pension law," and it specified that "the aid furnished shall be sufficient to enable the mothers to bring up their children in their own homes."[29]

In New York a bitter wrangle developed in 1912 between the advocates of public provision and those representing the COS viewpoint against public administration. When a widows' aid bill failed to pass the legislature, a state commission was appointed which submitted its report in 1914 with a "model bill." This passed in 1915 despite continued bitter opposition from the cos. Under its provisions New York followed the pattern of Pennsylvania in setting up separate county boards of child welfare outside the Poor Law system.[30]

Whatever the administrative arrangements selected by the various states and localities, they represented, conceptually, a break with the nineteenth-century insistence that widows had to struggle alone or else accept the almshouse for themselves and institutions or foster homes for their children, and thus separation from their youngsters. Hence many jurisdictions felt the need for workable guidelines for new administrative social controls that would meet the test of public approval. The fiscal area could be relatively precise; the resources and incomes of applicants as well as budgetary requirements could be stated in maximum or minimum terms, and the same was true of administrative organization and practice. Thanks to the research and educational work of the newly established United States Children's Bureau and the emerging professional knowledge in home economics, progress was made.[31]

Social criteria could not be so precise but were deemed essential to offset criticisms of such a drastic departure from entrenched customs and attitudes. People who focused primarily on children and advocated that any child in want should receive help were in a minority. Those who focused on family units tended to rely on the kind of restrictive requirements familiar to them in the selection of foster homes. In the post-Victorian period it was easy to apply to widows' aid the Poor Law of many states prohibiting giving relief to a family in which there was a male over fourteen capable of working. In only two northern states was there recognition of need among black families on a scale at all comparable with that for whites.[32]

Illness, especially tuberculosis, or bad housing, might lead to the home being classified unsuitable. Illegitimacy or other evidence of actual or potential "immoral" behavior, such as having a male boarder, made an applicant suspect to the point of almost certain rejection. Typical of the way such requirements were stated or implied in the laws was the Maine specification that an investigation should show whether the mother "is a fit and capable person to bring up her children, and whether the inmates and surroundings of her household are such as to render it suitable for her children to reside at home."[33]

If some of these requirements seem to us to have been subjective and judgmental, they were. It should be remembered, however, that in many places the decisions were to be made by judges who had available a substantial body of case law relating to adoptions and the care and custody of neglected and abused children in which these concepts were spelled out. Even where the decisions were made by lay persons, the legal precedents were well known.[34]

How did the cautious experiments fostered by the widows' pension movement work? The plans and administrative interpretations were so diverse that generalizations are dangerous. Most of the states enacted permissive legislation, leaving it up to local jurisdictions to put the statutes into operation. Almost always, it was the more change-oriented urban areas that took the lead in acting. More conservative rural areas tended to use traditional ways of identifying need and doing whatever they had been doing about it. Where the idea was taken up, its administrators were hemmed in by cultural, political, and economic realities. The larger objective of freeing mothers to maintain their previous levels of home life often was either lost sight of or rendered impossible to achieve.

Administrative and staffing arrangements at first were impromptu and ranged from the volunteer boards of women in Pennsylvania to the probation staffs of juvenile courts, oriented to the supervision of delinquent boys.[35] That situation was slow to change. Administrators pleaded for larger budgets not only to provide adequate aid to mothers but also to hire trained workers to administer the assistance. Failing in this, they turned to established private agencies to borrow staff and supervision and thus became captives of the very organizations that had fought most vigorously against publicly administered pensions.[36]

The funds appropriated were almost always totally inadequate. There was no standard way of dealing with this. In Pennsylvania some county boards chose to spread their allocations thinly so that all those eligible would get something. One enterprising county board improved on this by getting the relief authorities to match the pension granted each widow. In Philadelphia, however, where the board chose to give adequate relief or none, a long backlog of applicants went unserved. In 1918, the waiting list dated back to 1914.[37] When the cos, supporting the adequate relief policy of the public agency, refused to accept further cases of widows, the widespread need forced public attention and resulted in some additional funds.[38]

During 1915–16 the St. Louis Board of Childrens' Guardians maintained 210 children with their mothers, while the Provident Association aided 1,818 widows with families after they applied for relief.[39]

The penurious Poor Law orientation of the Board, reflecting widespread public attitudes, is revealed in the following vignettes of a few of the cases rejected between 1913 and 1916.[40]

> Inconsistencies in the data uncovered in the agent's investigation, together with a negative report from a church, overrode a favorable Children's Aid Society investigative report on a mother with nine children under fourteen years of age who was caring for her paralytic father and was herself thought to be suffering from cancer.
>
> The church thought the grandparents should continue to support a widow. The case was reopened and again rejected fifteen years later when the youngest child, apparently accepting the traditional system, applied to become a foster parent.
>
> Although the Board's agent recommended a supplemental grant of $5 a month, the fact that a widow earned $8 per week as a laundress during school hours made her children "not dependent on the public for support."
>
> The grinding effect of inadequate appropriations when a large increase in applications was expected meant that a family of five with earnings of $28 a month by the mother and $22 by a fourteen-year-old boy was refused a $6 grant "owing to the hard winter ahead" and "the amount involved was so small."
>
> A grandmother was ineligible because she was not a widow within the meaning of the law.
>
> The Board was not alone in lacking funds. The Provident Association (cos), answering a referral, declared, "Our funds are entirely exhausted and cannot place even one child."
>
> The effect on families of the inadequate funds and delays in making them available is seen in the record of a mother who had been seeking help for two years; in the final entry she released the children to the Board for foster care, for which there were adequate funds.

In spite of the blighting conditions such records reveal, and unfortunately the agency has destroyed all records that would show how families that did receive help fared, the widows' pension movement as a whole had positive results, even in those disorganized early years. It established the first effective reversal of the centuries-old denigration of public outdoor relief. The *St. Louis Star,* for instance, took up the cudgels "for a '100 percent' mother's pension law" when the Board rejected an obviously "worthy" case on the basis that an underage child could be excused from school to go to work.[41] An appreciable number of families were enabled to maintain a semblance of normality thanks to these measures, however inadequate they were by today's standards. Persons like Homer Folks who had accepted the cos opposition to public relief came to agree that the publicly administered funds did more good than harm, and there was increasing recognition that if the goals were to be reached state funding and enforcement would be required.

Widows' pensions brought into the open the magnitude of the problem. The cos had piously talked of the good it was doing for the limited group of "worthy" pensioners it supported. The general public had joined in consigning the remaining mass of those in need to the category of "unworthy" paupers. The cos had claimed the public administration would make aid a "right," which would attract great numbers of applicants who could, and should, find ways to survive without aid. In fact, wherever widows' pensions were introduced there was a flood of applications. Thus, the new programs brought to light in a dramatic way the extent of the misery the economic system was imposing and the inadequacies of the existing system of relief.[42] It also showed the economic as well as the social and moral importance of the child-caring role and bolstered the arguments of the advocates of social insurance, those who saw the pension as a necessary temporary provision until a more perfect, automatic system could be established.[43] Indeed, following the passage of the Social Security Act, experience under state-administered mothers' pensions programs provided telling arguments for the early addition of survivors insurance.

The widows' pension thus became another facet in the preventive efforts of the period. It created awareness of the problems of fatherless families. Typhoid fever, tuberculosis, and the venereal diseases were objects of sanitary and other public health measures. Industrial accidents and diseases inspired workmen's compensation and safety campaigns with notable results. The break-up of homes and family life due to poverty also called for preventive measures. The cos had demonstrated that positive results could be obtained in pilot projects with selected cases. Advocates of mothers' pensions sought to make these positive results more widely available. Their greatest shortcomings were failures to maintain public interpretation and effective pressure for the appropriations necessary for full implementation.[44] Nevertheless, the movement substituted new, more constructive sets of social controls for the older, more punitive and destructive ones, permanently reducing the number of institutionalized children.[45]

Piven and Cloward notwithstanding, no civil disorders prompted the alacrity with which widows' pensions took hold. The idea was initiated and promoted by vocal advocates for the prospective beneficiaries rather than by politicians, relief administrators, or the recipients themselves. There were no widespread protests on the part of women and children that might have induced appeasement by a new type of relief mechanism. In fact, deserted and widowed wives seem to have meekly accepted the prevailing mores that regarded women's place as the home, not the marketplace. These mothers were not politically motivated to challenge limitations of the marketplace that made replacement of their usual economic arrangements difficult if not impossible. Although nationwide statistics are hard to interpret because of the merging of mothers' pensions with the budgets of courts and with poor relief and other administrative units, there seems to have been little waxing and waning in response to the business cycle.

If the widows' aid movement illustrates any far-ranging systematic social response, it demonstrates how slowly basic changes in social structure occur. The advocates of the pensions were outraged by societal arrangements that broke up families for reasons of poverty alone and placed half-orphans whose mothers were willing to look after them in unsanitary almshouses, overcrowded orphanages, or foster homes. Their successes, weak and scattered as they were, represented the first break in centuries-old patterns of social provision. Prevention and genuine concern rather than amelioration and preservation of the free enterprise system were the objectives. This paved the way for the substantial, regular, assured income under the survivors insurance provisions of the Social Security Act now received by millions of full and half-orphans without a requirement that family life be disrupted by work. It paved the way also for the AFDC program, which, with all its faults, still compares favorably with what prevailed prior to World War I.[46]

NOTES

1. Frances F. Piven and Richard A. Cloward, *Regulating the Poor: The Functions of Public Welfare* (London: Vintage, 1972). The general thesis is stated on pp. 3–4. Mothers' (widows') pensions are specifically mentioned on pp. 48, 115–16, 128n, 134n, and 175–76.

2. The principal reference is Winifred Bell, *Aid to Dependent Children* (New York: Columbia Univ. Press, 1965). See *Regulating the Poor,* 175–76.

3. Josephine Shaw Lowell, "The Economic and Moral Effects of Public Outdoor Relief," *Proceedings of the National Conference of Charities and Correction* [hereafter cited as *NCCC*], *1890,* (Boston: George H. Ellis, 1891), 81–91; Samuel Smiles, *Self Help* (Nashville, Tenn.: A.H. Redord, 1873).

4. The economic contribution of homemaking and the current social values attached to it were recognized in Edward T. Devine, *Principles of Relief* (New York: Macmillan, 1905), 91–92: "In the normal family the contribution made by the mother to the common welfare is fully equal to that of the father. The loss of the mother may well be held to reduce by one-half the effective income of the family, even though she does not earn a dollar of money." For typical contemporary descriptions of the plight of widows, see Florence Kelly, "Industrial Causes of Juvenile Delinquency," *NCCC, 1905* (n.p.: Fred J. Heer, 1906), 148–49; Edward T. Devine, *Misery and Its Causes* (New York: Macmillan, 1913), 187–88; Belle Linder Israels, "Widowed Mothers," *The Survey* 22 (4 Sept. 1909), 741; Jane Addams, "Charity and Social Justice," *NCCC, 1910* (Fort Wayne: Fort Wayne Printing Co., 1911), 6–8.

5. Commonwealth of Massachusetts, "*Report* of the Commission on the Support of Dependent Minor Children of Widowed Mothers, January, 1913," in Emma O. Lundberg, *Unto the Least of These* (New York: D. Appleton-Century, 1947), 127.

6. Quoted in Edward T. Devine, *The Principles of Relief,* 94. In this paper, "cos" is used as a general term to designate the "scientific charity" approach in which charity organization societies were the leaders.

7. Charles Richmond Henderson, *Introduction to the Study of Dependent, Defective and Delinquent Classes And Their Social Treatment* (Boston: D.C. Heath, 1893), 98.

8. Michael W. Sherraden, "Institutionalization of Children and Youth in the United States, Colonial Times to 1970," unpublished paper, University of Michigan, Doctoral Program in Social Work and Social Science, (March 1977), 50.

9. "Statistics of Institution Inmates," *NCCC, 1908* (Fort Wayne: Ft. Wayne Printing Co., 1909), 42–43.

10. Edward T. Devine, "Pensions for Mothers," (1913) in Robert H. Bremner, et al., eds., *Children and Youth in America,* 3 Vols. (Cambridge, Mass.: Harvard Univ. Press, 1971), 2: 377–79. See also I.M. Rubinow, *Social Insurance* (New York: H. Holt, 1913), 436–38, and *The Quest for Security* (New York: H. Holt, 1934), 498–99.

11. For advocates of widows' pensions, see Mark H. Leff, "The Mothers' Pension Movement in the Progressive Era," *Social Service Review* 37 (Sept. 1973), 405–10.

12. *Proceedings of the White House Conference on the Care of Dependent Children* (Washington, D.C.: G. P. O., 1909), 9–14. For contemporary use of similar phrases and principles for the selection of foster homes, see George Harrison Durand, "The Study of the Child from the Standpoint of the Home-Finding Agency," *NCCC, 1907* (Indianapolis: William B. Buford, 1908), 260.

13. "Third Biennial Report of the Department of Social Welfare of the

State of California, July 1, 1930 to June 30, 1932," in Grace Abbott, ed., *The Child and the State,* 2 Vols. (Chicago: Univ. of Chicago Press, 1938), 2: 107–8. Apparently this provision was little used until after 1904, when Dr. Walter Lindley, dean of the College of Medicine, University of Southern California, and president of the Board of Trustees of the Whittier State School, lamented the more than five thousand children in state institutions, two-thirds of whom were half-orphans, and advocated an organized effort to assist poor widows. "The Evils of Institutional Childhood." *NCCC, 1905* (n.p.: Fred J. Heer, 1906, 125–28.

14. Franklin B. Sanborn, "Indoor and Outdoor Relief," *NCCC, 1890* (Boston: George H. Ellis, 1891), 71–80; Josephine Shaw Lowell, "The Economic and Moral Effects of Public Outdoor Relief," *NCCC, 1890* (Boston: George H. Ellis, 1891), 81–91.

15. Amos G. Warner, *American Charities* (New York: Crowell, 1894), 174.

16. *Charities Review* 8 (Jan. 1899), 499. A description of the operation from *Charities* 7 (1901) is in Bremner et al., eds., *Children and Youth in America,* 2: 353–55. Comments on it are in Frank Dekker Watson, *The Charity Organization Movement in the United States* (New York: Macmillan, 1922), 393–99.

17. Homer Folks, *The Care of Destitute, Neglected and Delinquent Children* (New York: Macmillan, 1907), 176.

18. In December 1912, the New York Association for Improving the Condition of the Poor started an experiment with aid to fifty widows that was so successful that in 1914 it was extended to all widows in its care. John Lewis Gillin, *Poverty and Dependency* (New York: D. Appleton-Century, 1937), 176. For cos reaction to enactment of widows' pensions, see the debate between Merritt W. Pinckney, judge of the Cook County Juvenile Court, and Frederick Almy, secretary of the Buffalo cos, together with the subsequent discussion, *NCCC, 1912* (Fort Wayne: Ft. Wayne Printing Co., 1913), 473–98. Other opponents are described in Leff, "The Mothers' Pension Movement," 402–3.

19. Galen A. Merrill, "Some Recent Developments in Child Saving," *NCCC, 1900* (Boston: George H. Ellis, 1901), 228.

20. Sweat-shop conditions and early scholarship plans are described in Owen R. Lovejoy, "Child Labor and Philanthropy," *NCCC, 1907* (Indianapolis: William B. Buford, 1908) 203. For Oklahoma legislation see Lundberg, *Unto the Least of These,* 124.

21. For an early exposition of the needs of Chicago children being dealt with by private charity and the juvenile court, see Sherman C. Kingsley, "Public Dependents and the State," *NCCC, 1905* (n.p.: Fred J. Heer, 1906), 394–403. In her NCCC presidential address, Jane Addams dramatically presented the need for state assistance to widowed mothers in their own homes. See *NCCC, 1910* (Fort Wayne: Ft. Wayne Printing Co., 1911), 6–8.

22. Grace Abbott, "Mothers' Aid: Introduction" in Abbott, *The Child and the State,* 2: 229–31.

23. *The Survey* 26 (15 April 1911), 105; George B. Mangold, *The Challenge of St. Louis* (New York: Missionary Education Movement, 1917) 137; Alfred Fairbanks, "Mothers' Pensions in Missouri," *NCCC, 1914* (Fort

Wayne: Ft. Wayne Printing Co., 1915), 444; James Lieby, *Charity and Correction in New Jersey* (New Brunswick, N.J.: Rutgers Univ. Press, 1967), 94–95; Amos W. Butler, "Adequate Relief to Needy Mothers in Indiana," *NCCC, 1914* (Fort Wayne: Ft. Wayne Printing Co., 1915), 440–41.

24. Emma O. Lundberg and Mary E. Milburn, *Child Dependency in the District of Columbia* (New York: Negro Univ. Press, 1969), 102–6.

25. Mary F. Bogue, "Problems in the Administration of Mothers' Aid," *NCCC, 1918* (Chicago: Rogers and Hall, 1919), 349–55.

26. Leiby, *Charity and Correction,* 96.

27. See footnote 13.

28. Stanley H. Howe, "Adequate Relief to Needy Mothers in Pennsylvania," *NCCC, 1914* (Fort Wayne: Ft. Wayne Printing Co., 1915), 447–50; Bogue, "Problems in the Administration," 349–59.

29. Frank W. Goodhue, "Problems of Administration of Mothers' Aid: Discussion," *NCCC, 1918* (Chicago: Rogers and Hall, 1919), 365, italics in the original. See also David F. Tilley, "Adequate Relief to Mothers in Massachusetts," *NCCC, 1914* (Fort Wayne: Ft. Wayne Printing Co., 1915), 453–55.

30. Lundberg, *Unto the Least of These,* 129–30. Bremner et al., eds., *Children and Youth in America,* 2: 379–84, 398–410, gives the commission report and reactions to increasing criticisms of institutions.

31. Florence Nesbit, "The Family Budget and its Supervision," *NCCC, 1918* (Chicago: Rogers and Hall, 1919), 359–65; Lundberg and Milburn, *Child Dependency,* 101–9.

32. United States Children's Bureau, *Mother's Aid, 1931,* in Bremner et al., eds., *Children and Youth in America,* 2: 396.

33. Lundberg and Milburn, *Child Dependency,* 108.

34. Bremner et al., eds., *Children and Youth in America,* "The Legal Status of Children and Protection Against Cruelty and Immorality," 2: 115–246.

35. Howe, "Adequate Relief," 448; Bogue, "Problems in the Administration," 358; Pinckney, *NCCC, 1912* (Fort Wayne: Ft. Wayne Printing Co., 1913), 475–97.

36. "Since [an experienced COS worker] . . . has come in we are making good use of excellent volunteers that come to us unsought." Gertrude Vaile to Porter Lee, 27 September 1916, in Ralph E. Pumphrey and Muriel W. Pumphrey, eds., *The Heritage of American Social Work* (New York: Columbia Univ. Press, 1961), 339. Miss Vaile, a student of Mary Richmond, was attempting to apply COS principles in her administration of the public assistance activities, including widows' pensions, of the Denver Department of Social Welfare. In "The Mothers' Pension Movement," Mark Leff states "it would be unfair to equate the operation envisioned by mothers' pension advocates with the practices of the social caseworkers who obtained an ever-tightening grip on this program."

37. Bogue, "Problems in the Administration," 350.

38. Watson, *The Charity Organization Movement,* 137.

39. Mangold, *Challenge of St. Louis,* 137. The Provident Association was the COS type organization in St. Louis.

40. All early records of accepted cases and most records of rejected cases have been destroyed by the agency. By chance a small, unscientific sam-

pling of cases rejected between 1913 and 1933 were saved and are now preserved as "Board of Children's Guardians Records" in the University Archives, Olin Library, Washington University in St. Louis, Mo. All cases mentioned are from Box I.

41. Ibid., Box I, File 212.54.

42. In the discussion following the 1912 debate over the Illinois law (see Note 18 above), Homer Folks, who had drafted the White House Conference *Report,* was so impressed by the arguments of the Chicago judge that he commented, "I am not so sure in the case of widows that it is not a matter of right after all. A feeling of reliance upon a steady and regular income ought to be a good thing." See *NCCC, 1912* (Fort Wayne: Ft. Wayne Printing Co., 1913), 486–87. He later became a staunch advocate of publicly financed pensions. See Walter I. Trattner, *Homer Folks* (New York: Columbia Univ. Press, 1968), 114–15.

43. Mary Van Kleek, "Women's Work—A Problem of Poverty," *Charity Organization Bulletin* (Oct. 1912), 201–5; I.M. Rubinow, *Social Insurance,* 435–36.

44. I.M. Rubinow, *The Quest for Security,* 488; Jane Addams, *The Spirit of Youth and the City Streets* (New York: Macmillan, 1909), 149–50.

45. Walter I. Trattner, *From Poor Law to Welfare State* (New York: Free Press, 1974), 190; Leff, "The Mothers' Pension Movement," 414.

46. Since this was written in the winter of 1979–80, the resurgence of traditional attitudes calling for individual, as against collective, responsibility has culminated in massive attacks on nearly all social support programs. Notable here have been those on AFDC, Supplemental Security Income (SSI) and survivor and disability benefits under Social Security. Far from following the Piven/Cloward argument that the programs prop up a low-wage structure, high officials of the national administration argue that these programs deter recipients from seeking work.

THE FORMATIVE YEARS OF SOCIAL SECURITY:

A Test Case of the Piven and Cloward Thesis

W. ANDREW ACHENBAUM

Carnegie-Mellon University

In 1971, Frances Fox Piven and Richard A. Cloward, then professors of political science and of sociology at Columbia University's School of Social Work, published *Regulating the Poor*. The book elaborated upon ideas about the functions of public welfare that the authors first presented in a series of influential essays in *The Nation,* and it developed insights they had gained while participating in several anti-poverty movements at the grassroots level.[1] *Regulating the Poor,* however, was not a personal reminiscence of the rise and fall of the Great Society programs. It was neither an administrative critique nor a polemical prescription for radical reforms of "the System," although the writers' sense of outrage over contemporary social injustices clearly colored their argument. Rather, the work was a fresh, thought-provoking analysis of continuities and changes in the rationale for and the methods of providing public relief, which focused on developments in the United States during the middle of the twentieth century.

Piven and Cloward rejected a "whiggish" interpretation of social welfare history. They challenged interpretations that contended that governmental social policies, at any level, have become more and more responsible, responsive, or munificent in dealing with poor people's needs over time. In their opinion, public welfare has performed and continues to accomplish a broader social function: "Historical evidence suggests that relief arrangements are initiated or expanded during the occasional outbreaks of civil disorder produced by mass unemployment, and are then abolished or contracted when political stability is restored. We shall argue that expansive relief policies are designed to mute civil disorder, and restrictive ones to reinforce work norms. In other words, relief policies are cyclical—liberal or restrictive depending on the problems of regulation in the larger society with which government must contend."[2]

Regulating the Poor — as the title itself suggested — rested on a model of social control. According to Piven and Cloward, public officials increase benefits and expand services to the needy in order to placate and pacify groups who might otherwise fundamentally alter the prevailing balance of power and resources amid times of social unrest or economic uncertainty. Under more economically favorable conditions in society at large, however, those in charge usually do not feel terribly threatened by potential malcontents. This permits a reduction in relief rolls, leaving on the welfare rolls only those whose economic value is deemed so marginal that it makes more sense to permit them *not* to work. Thus, in good times and bad, the power elite governs as it sees fit. The needs and desires of the poor, on the other hand, are taken seriously only when they absolutely must be. Generally, the poor are ignored, coerced, appeased, and controlled as circumstances warrant.

Upon publication, *Regulating the Poor* was both admired and damned for its radical interpretation of public welfare as much as for its intellectual content. Piven and Cloward's portrayal of mass/elite relationships, which stressed, as Michael Harrington put it in a review of the work, "force on the part of the underclass and chicanery on the part of the ruling class"[3] in explaining pivotal moments in American welfare history, appealed to many because it complemented prevailing New Left perspectives on the Cold War and seemed to be confirmed by Nixon's domestic and foreign policies. Furthermore, eminent social scientists and policy experts such as Herbert Gans, Robert Merton, and Alvin Schorr praised the authors' breadth and style; Peter Steinfels claimed that "no future discussion can afford to ignore them."[4] *Regulating the Poor* won the C. Wright Mills Award of the Society for the Study of Social Problems in 1971. But the book's bold thesis also provoked some controversy and was sharply criticized by a few reviewers, who complained that key terms were poorly defined, the model reductionist, and the analysis sloppy. Lance Liebman, writing in the *Harvard Law Review,* concluded, "The evidence is interesting, the generalizations crude, and in the end, dull."[5]

Nevertheless, a decade after its publication, although still debated, the thesis presented in *Regulating the Poor* remains widely cited. Indeed, Piven and Cloward's characterization of public welfare as an instrument of social control has been elevated to an article of faith on the American Left.[6] Regardless of how one views its ideological merits, however, the work is worth reading for its conceptual framework as much as for its provocative thesis. Piven and Cloward clearly have advanced our understanding of the functions of public welfare by treating the relief system as an institution intimately connected to other institutions. They offer a holistic model for approaching social welfare that moves us beyond most available frameworks. They posit interrelationships between the purposes of relief and the political process, the occupational and class structure, market incentives, social order and violence, religious customs, and philosophical tenets. Seeking out the larger structural/cultural causes and effects of particular governmental welfare policies enables Piven and Cloward to ask "big questions" and, in so doing, to elucidate the dynamics of American society.

Furthermore, an interest in changing societal dynamics *over time* as well as at any precise moment enhances the descriptive and explanatory powers of *Regulating the Poor*. Piven and Cloward display a genuine concern for determining whether a historical episode is the unique product of a special set of ecological and temporal circumstances or whether it fits into patterns observed in other places and at other times. Their analysis evokes neither a "golden age" we have lost nor a pre-industrial abyss we have surmounted. Nor is theirs a homogenized recounting: group conflict, incompatible perceptions of reality, and societal dysfunctions all figure prominently in the authors' discussion of Elizabethan practices and other pre-twentieth-century American precedents. Because they realize that the past is not the present writ small, Piven and Cloward try to describe successive expansions and contractions of relief measures in terms consistent with the periods that created them. Thus, their claim that there is a cyclical pattern in the ways that governments give relief does not necessarily presuppose a crudely mechanistic model of societal change impervious to the contrarieties and surprises manifest in the historical record. Quite the contrary. Applying their model requires one to look within a rigorously delineated historical framework for specific sources of societal dislocation, unequivocal evidence of civil turbulence, and concrete governmental responses, which were directly followed by overt popular repercussions. Used in this way, their model appears to have predictive as well as heuristic merit. And so it does.

In fact, it is the potential applicability of Piven and Cloward's conceptual model for forecasting developments in public welfare that makes *Regulating the Poor* so significant. For if the authors have succeeded in retrospectively predicting the broad contours of the Great Society on the basis of their analysis of the New Deal, then one feels fairly confident in extending their longitudinal baseline and relying on it to assess the relative value of possible scenarios for the years ahead. Indeed, events during the past decade have confirmed rather than undermined their thesis that governments typically transfer a large proportion of the poor from direct relief to work-related relief. One might plausibly interpret various work-incentive provisions in the Ford, Carter, and Reagan welfare reform proposals in this manner.

Yet, while Piven and Cloward's thesis seems increasingly credible in the short run, paradoxically, its long-term historical validity remains untested. Reviewers to date have concentrated on the authors' treatment of the 1960s; few have offered any sustained criticism of the historical sections of the book or suggested that historical episodes not covered in the work call into question its thesis. To the best of my knowledge, *Regulating the Poor* was reviewed in only two major historical journals, and, even then, it merely received passing notice.[7] Far from signaling an unwillingness to take multidisciplinary studies by non-professional historians seriously, the neglect of Piven and Cloward's work reflects the preeminence of different research interests within the historical community since World War II. Historians now, however, are producing monographs in the field of social welfare history that, when considered in conjunction with earlier administrative case studies and biographies, would permit a judicious critique of *Regulating the Poor* as a socio-cultural interpretation of American welfare history.

I do not propose to offer such a definitive review here. Instead, the bulk of this essay is an exploration of a single issue crucial to the overall thesis in *Regulating the Poor,* one that should stimulate further reflections on social-control models in general: Did the passage of the Social Security Act constitute, as Piven and Cloward argue, a deliberate effort on the part of the Roosevelt administration to regulate the aged poor? I conclude with some comments on how future research into the formative years of Social Security can build upon *Regulating the Poor* without necessarily endorsing all aspects of its authors' argument or slighting the humanitarian impulse expressed at the time. I hope that this essay will demonstrate the importance of factually accurate historical analysis in evaluating welfare options, particularly for the aging and the aged in the future.

Piven and Cloward's interpretation of "Relief and the Great Depression," a two-chapter analysis that makes up Part One of their book, conforms neatly to their overarching thesis about the origins and purposes of public welfare in America. They begin their analysis by claiming that "the first major relief crisis in the United States occurred during the Great Depression."[8] To corroborate this point, they marshall an impressive array of statistics and first-hand reports documenting the extent of mass unemployment, bank closures, and tight money that wreaked havoc on farmers and urban families. They also point out that agencies in the private sector and public ones at the local level were overwhelmed by requests for relief and that the Hoover administration was unwilling to provide vital assistance to the needy.

According to Piven and Cloward's model, however, widespread destitution per se is a necessary but not a sufficient cause for expanding welfare rolls. The sine qua non of welfare reform is the outburst of civil disorder, which in turn causes a marked behavioral shift among the electorate. Finding appropriate evidence to satisfy this aspect of their model is no problem: Piven and Cloward describe instances of violence in Chicago, Detroit, and New York City and recount the 1932 protest of the Bonus Expeditionary Force, which ended in the shadow of the Capitol as federal troops marched on the disgruntled veterans' camp.[9] The authors then review the results of the election of 1932, noting the significant increase in voter turnout and the wide margin of Roosevelt's plurality.

In the next phase of their analysis, Piven and Cloward focus on the expansion of direct relief once Roosevelt was inaugurated. They emphasize that the Federal Emergency Relief Administration was unprecedented in affirming the federal government's responsibility to the needy and, relatively speaking, in responding to poor people's needs. Various efforts in 1932 and 1933 to initiate work relief and to appeal to business leaders also are described. By 1934, however, Roosevelt realized that his source of political strength derived from labor and ethnic groups in the North, farmers, and the traditionally Democratic South; he recognized that business organizations opposed him. Accordingly, the President sought "to cement his constituency" and to undercut insurgency within the fledgling New Deal coalition, especially among groups representing the unemployed and the aged.[10] At this juncture, the narrative suggests that the way that Roosevelt tried to regulate the aged poor was by co-opting them.

The elderly's interests, the authors indicate, were embodied in a movement founded by Dr. Francis E. Townsend in 1934 in Long Beach, California. Townsend proposed that all Americans over sixty be given a monthly pension of two hundred dollars on the condition that they not work and that they spend the entire amount within thirty days. The California physician and sometime real-estate agent quickly mobilized tremendous support for this measure. Citing evidence in Abraham Holtzman's *The Townsend Movement* (1963), Arthur Schlesinger's *The Politics of Upheaval* (1960), a sociologist's 1955 essay on the decline of the Townsendites, and a 1935 article in *The Nation,* Piven and Cloward report that the movement grew from several hundred thousand supporters in 1934 — a number sufficiently large, it is pointed out, to intimidate congressmen discussing a Townsend Plan bill — to several million in 1936.[11] Such widespread support reflected not only the increasing proportion of older people — whose percentage of the total population had doubled since 1900 — in desperate straits because of the Depression but also the growing conviction among Americans that something had to be done to remedy the situation.

Either to defuse the clamor or to win votes, or both, Roosevelt called for strong congressional action to provide federal relief for the aged. "What the old folks got instead — and if it did not entirely placate them, it placated their public supporters — was the Social Security legislation. This meager legislative concession spelled the demise of the movement, but the Townsendites did not give up without a long fight," according to Piven and Cloward.[12] The passage of the Social Security Act in 1935, in their view, signaled only a token victory for aged insurgents. It was, however, as much as they were going to realize in the 1930s. The enactment of old-age relief, we are told, quelled agitation on behalf of the elderly. The election of 1936, moreover, sealed the fate of extremist groups who had hoped to press for more expansive welfare measures. Buoyed by the returns, Roosevelt saw no need to make additional concessions.

Hence, after 1936, argue Piven and Cloward, "reforms" of the federal relief program led to a contraction of welfare benefits for needy groups, including the elderly. Social Security remained on the books, of course, but various provisions written into the original act and subsequent amendments had the cumulative effect of keeping the number of elderly workers eligible for benefits low. The federal government also permitted state and local agencies considerable leeway in designing and administering their programs; most states exerised their prerogative and established low levels of aid to the aged poor.[13] Other groups (such as the able-bodied unemployed), the authors note, felt the effects of cutbacks more severely than did the old. Nevertheless, Piven and Cloward contend that the classic cyclical expansion/contraction pattern affected the aged's welfare benefits, too.

On the surface, the interpretation of the formative years of Social Security set forth in *Regulating the Poor* seems eminently plausible. There *was* a Depression, which was long and severe. Furthermore, older Americans had evinced little interest in organizing as a self-conscious, politically savvy group for any purpose prior to the 1930s: they certainly had never before represented either a significant threat to domestic tranquility or a voting bloc that needed to be satisfied. It is reasonable to suppose that there is an intimate connection, therefore, between the rise of the Townsendites in 1934 and the passage of Social Security a year later. And it makes sense that the passage of *any* measure would have placated, to at least a politically tolerable level, public demands for the government to do something for the elderly. Thus, given the decisiveness of Roosevelt's landslide in 1936, it is not wholly surprising that the administration no longer felt overwhelming political pressure to raise taxes and possibly disrupt economic recovery in order to give the aged poor some additional benefits.

Unfortunately, what seems so clear on the surface becomes terribly murky once one investigates a bit more deeply. Indeed, Piven and Cloward's analyses of the impact of the Depression, of the merging New Deal coalition of insurgents, of the significance of the Townsendites in particular, of the forces motivating Roosevelt to act in the way he did, and of the basic provisions and initial impact of the Social Security Act itself are flawed in varying degrees. Let us consider each of their interpretations in turn.

As for the impact of the Depression, Piven and Cloward are surely correct in arguing that the original purpose and scope of the Social Security Act cannot be fully understood without recognizing that the measure was created in the midst of a severe economic crisis. But, by pressing the point too hard, they misstate the significance of the Great Depression. At the conclusion of a seven-paragraph historical synopsis of relief practices in the United States before 1930, for instance, we are told: "When the Great Depression struck in the 1930s, there were only those local relief arrangements, virtually unchanged since colonial times, to deal with the disaster. All the old methods—from almshouse to indentured service—were still in use. In many places, private charities were the sole resource for the destitute."[14]

This summary suggests more continuities in American social welfare history from 1607 to 1929 (and encourages the reader to anticipate more dramatic discontinuities wrought by the Depression) than was the case. Piven and Cloward's interpretation overlooks the rise of professional standards in the late nineteenth century as well as the impact of the Progressive era's confidence in the salutary, parental role of the State—phenomena that many scholars contend fundamentally altered the focus, outlook, and methods prevailing in the welfare arena.[15] They also ignore late-nineteenth- and early-twentieth-century efforts in both the public and private sectors to *prevent* old-age pauperism by providing retirement pensions and life insurance annuities. The indirect—but significant—effect that veterans' programs had on reducing the likelihood that former soldiers and sailors and their dependents would become impoverished in later life receives no mention.[16] And although the authors are quick to point out the inadequacies of various state relief programs, it also should be noted that *no* federal-state relief arrangements could have been established in the 1930s without the *prior* creation of bureaucratic networks at the state and federal levels.[17] Had they incorporated the preceding factors into their analysis, Piven and Cloward may have been less inclined to interpret New Deal approaches to the problem of relief as such an abrupt break with the past.

Piven and Cloward also exaggerate the extent to which the Depression caused the status of the aged to deteriorate rapidly. Their use of statistics to make their case is misleading. I would like to know how they determined that the incidence of old-age dependency rose from 30 percent to 50 percent between 1928 and 1935.[18] If their figures are correct, then it would indeed appear that the Depression had a devastating impact. Yet the historical record actually precludes such precision: researchers offered estimates of old-age poverty during the 1920s that ranged from 16 to 66 percent; government officials in 1935 assumed that about 50 percent of all older people needed assistance, but they were not sure.[19] Hence, while elderly Americans obviously suffered greatly in the 1930s, their overall economic situation had been problematic for decades. What the Depression did was to extend the web of poverty and economic vulnerability, thereby entrapping large numbers of middle-class citizens who had presumed themselves sufficiently prepared for the financial vicissitudes of later years.

The really significant connection between the Great Depression and the passage of the Social Security Act, as far as the aged are concerned, is that the crisis tragically resolved serious reservations Americans had expressed about the need for federal assistance and insurance programs for the nation's older citizens, ideas that had been debated in the press and in Congress for at least two decades. As more and more Americans suffered prolonged economic hardship, the predicament of the aged and the inadequacy of existing relief sources became indisputable. Consequently, it at last seemed feasible to consider seriously a federal welfare program. But it is worth speculating that some sort of national plan would have been implemented anyway. Between 1927 and 1932 (that is, before the full impact of the Depression had been felt), there was a significant increase in organized pressure for, and a noticeable decrease in philosophical and political opposition to, such a scheme. Hence, the Depression experience accelerated developments already taking shape in the social welfare arena. The crisis should not be viewed as the fount of radically new ideas or activities.

With regard to the emerging New Deal coalition of "insurgents," Piven and Cloward's failure to put the Depression experience into proper historical perspective taints the rest of their interpretation. Examine, for instance, their analysis of the ways that various segments of American society reacted to adverse conditions in the early 1930s. Because the authors overstate the social dislocations wrought by the economic crisis, they are too simplistic in depicting the nature and dynamics of popular discontent: "As the Depression wore on, with conditions showing little improvement, unrest resurfaced. By 1934, various dissident leaders were drawing upon this unrest, giving it organizational form and coherence, aspiring to build political movements that would change the face of America. For, after five years of hardship and confusion, anything seemed possible, and saints and opportunists, reformists and revolutionaries, right wing and left — all thought to grasp the moment to shape the future of America."[20]

Hard times, unrest, uncertainty, and instability, Piven and Cloward claim, provided a propitious milieu for advocating and demanding significant changes in the status quo. They identify pivotal reform-minded groups — militants in organized labor, Huey Long's followers, organizations of and for the unemployed, Townsendites, Coughlinites — and point out that the quality and style of these groups' leaders differed profoundly.[21] Still, in the authors' opinion, differences among the organizations seem less salient than the fact that each group articulated a new "American dream" and that, in the end, each met a similar fate.

Lumping under the broad category of "insurgents" the diverse concerns and activities of persons pressing for old-age pensions, of militant labor groups demanding better wages and collective-bargaining privileges, and of ad-hoc coalitions of unemployed workers insisting on jobs is unwarranted, however, for it confounds too many issues. Just because each of these groups felt hard-pressed and wanted changes does not mean that they shared common philosophies or strategies. Different sets of people may simultaneously bemoan or condemn the same set of conditions for very different reasons and with different degrees of intensity. Opposition to "x" does not invariably lead to support for "y."

Indeed, Piven and Cloward never really demonstrate that all dissident groups diagnosed what was wrong with America, much less that they prescribed what should be done next, in a complementary manner. The narrative tells how Roosevelt hoped to rebuild the economy, enhance occupational roles, and restore familial and community ties through relief, recovery, and reform.[22] But does it necessarily follow that the insurgents perceived the sources of unrest in the same way as did the President? Were those out of work primarily disturbed by *temporary* unemployment or *any* type of unemployment? If the former, were they equally concerned about the plight of the unskilled factory worker, the migrant farmer, and the skilled craftsman? If the latter, did they mention able-bodied women, blacks, and men over fifty or sixty, or did they really focus on the plight of able-bodied, young and middle-aged, white unemployed men? *Regulating the Poor* does not entertain such questions. Yet there is a large body of literature that shows that supporters of publicly funded unemployment insurance disagreed, among other things, over identifying whom within the ranks of the "unemployed" deserved or required assistance.[23] Similarly, commentators in the late 1920s and 1930s did not agree in their assessments of the needs of the "aged." Some thought that all older Americans should be assisted; others wanted to limit relief to those who were poor. Still others asserted that a potential recipient's marital status and the number of kin obliged to care for an elderly person should be taken into consideration.

In short, the authors ignore a key element in the socio-political chemistry of the New Deal coalition by emphasizing similarities and parallel efforts and by glossing over disagreements and rivalries, not simply within dissident organizations but also among various interest groups. This oversight makes it impossible for them to deal in a sophisticated manner with the struggle to enact unemployment insurance at the state and federal level. And, as we shall now see, it introduces distortions into their discussion of the "gray lobby."

Piven and Cloward exaggerate the significance of the Townsendites. In fact, they miss an opportunity to assess the growing philosophical and organizational pressure wielded by different groups that lobbied for old-age pensions in the 1920s and 1930s by analyzing *only* the contributions made by the Townsendites and, after 1936, their allies in the Union party. While the authors rightly pointed out that Townsend created the largest old people's protest movement, they overestimated the group's significance because they relied too heavily on Abraham Holtzman's contention that Townsendite pressure led to the inclusion of an old-age insurance provision in the Social Security Act.[24] There is considerable evidence to suggest otherwise. Moderate commentators at the time clearly had grave reservations about the effectiveness of Townsend's scheme and questioned the leader's cost/benefit figures.[25] Furthermore, officials intimately involved in the passage of Social Security as well as later analysts tend to discount the Townsendites' contributions, because they appeared on the scene "too late to decisively effect the course of legislative development."[26]

Indeed, one could make a far stronger case for the vital role in securing Social Security played by two rival groups that are not even mentioned in *Regulating the Poor*. On the one hand, there was the American Association for Labor Legislation (AALL), which after World War I began to advocate protective old-age insurance plans through collective bargaining demands and business cooperation. Several AALL members held key staff positions on the executive committee that drew up the 1935 old-age legislation. On the other hand, there was the American Association for Old Age Security (AAOAS), which was founded in 1927 and supported the use of social insurance as a means of cushioning the inevitable tragedies of life and, more boldly, as a way of redistributing income. The organization's chief spokesman, Abraham Epstein, did not help to draft Social Security legislation, but his views were influential.[27] That both of these groups were active before the Townsend movement arose and that they both endorsed government supervision of social insurance undercut the persuasiveness of Piven and Cloward's argument. Furthermore, the marked difference between the AALL and the AAOAS suggests issues ignored by the authors. The alternatives before the nation were not simply what the Townsendites demanded and what Social Security ultimately delivered. Clearly, there were at least two other perspectives on the ways social insurance could be used and financed. And there were other matters to debate. Should the federal government require that all workers contribute to the system, or should the program be run on a voluntary basis? Should insurance and assistance programs be established in tandem or should they be separated? Opinions on these and other matters differed widely in the early 1930s.[28] Such lack of consensus, even among those who thought that the federal government should venture into this area in the first place, forced policy makers to make tough choices that they knew would disappoint everybody in some of the particulars and probably satisfy no one completely.

Just as Piven and Cloward ignore the wide range of organized support for old-age pensions as well as the fundamental incompatibility of many of the specific provisions such groups advocated, so too they slight some key factors that influenced the President in timing and shaping his Social Security legislation. Their claim that Roosevelt "emphasized themes calculated to assuage the discontent spawned by economic catastrophe" and "to contain . . . dissident movements and to consolidate them behind the New Deal"[29] is accurate as far as it goes, but it does not go far enough. To maintain power, Roosevelt obviously needed to confront the vital issues of the day and keep his current and potential supporters satisfied. Yet shrewd leaders must do more than get a sense of the nation's drift and then manipulate it to their best advantage. As James MacGregor Burns observed:

> Effective policy makers — those working for real change — must move
> on directly and purposely to . . . assess the impact of policies that,
> in satisfying existing and recognizable need, alter the motivations not
> simply by extinguishing them and returning them to some kind of equi-

librium *but that in the very act of satisfaction create further wants and demands.* And they must calculate, if they can, what hierarchical order of needs and values may activate "higher" stages. The policy maker must anticipate reactions from informal and unofficial leaders as well as from formal ones and in a variety of settings and circumstances, not only the structural and traditional ones. Thus, it was necessary for Roosevelt to move on from the economic "survival" needs of the "first" New Deal of 1933 to the egalitarian and reformist requirements of the "second" New Deal of 1935.[30]

Burns provides a more useful framework than the one presented in *Regulating the Poor* for explicating the various factors that motivated and constrained Roosevelt. His framework enables us to appreciate the difficulties in getting any social security legislation enacted, especially a measure designed to satisfy immediate needs and to address long-term goals.

Following Burns's cues, for example, one might argue that Roosevelt called for old-age relief in 1935, not primarily in response to insurgent Townsendites, but mainly in keeping with his judgment that the right time had come. After all, Roosevelt could have acted earlier: it is important to note that he had been instrumental in securing passage in 1929 of the nation's most generous old-age-assistance program while serving as governor of New York (a fact, incidentally, not mentioned by Piven and Cloward), and he had been urged by fellow Democrats to lend his support to several assistance measures introduced in Congress between 1932 and 1935. But Roosevelt chose to wait until the economy had begun to recover and until the first round of public and congressional discussion had placed the debate over various old-age proposals into sharper focus. Yet even when the administration decided to move, Roosevelt and his advisers faced serious obstacles that had impeded earlier attempts to involve the federal government in a publicly funded program of old-age assistance or in social and unemployment insurance schemes.[31] Policy makers lacked the data necessary to determine how many elderly people needed help and how much help they needed. They faced significant pressure from groups on the extreme left and right whose opposition to programs that did too much or too little might be modulated but never muted. Whatever compromises were reached, in fact, not only had to make sense philosophically and politically but also to be feasible economically and defensible constitutionally.

Drafting a social security bill into a workable policy thus required molding an amalgam of new and old practices and ideas in a politically and socio-economically volatile atmosphere. That Roosevelt's measure gained overwhelming approval from the public, constructive criticism from knowledgeable reformers who were disappointed with aspects of the final product, and constitutional support from the Supreme Court attests to the President's good luck, uncanny knack for forging unlikely alliances and securing unexpected cooperation, and capacity to lead, not just his political shrewdness. But we would never know this from reading *Regulating the Poor.*

Furthermore, although Piven and Cloward's brief comments about Social Security are fully consistent with their overall hypothesis, their description misrepresents the original provisions and completely disregards the important 1939 amendments. A careful reading of the text reveals that old-age assistance (Title I) and old-age insurance provisions (Title II) were included in the 1935 bill. (Title I was designed to relieve those older people currently in need; Title II was intended to reduce the extent of old-age dependency by enabling workers to make provisions for their later years.) But the authors make no effort to explain how the system was supposed to work. At some points, in fact, Piven and Cloward write as if relief measures were not coordinated with insurance measures.

On page 101 of *Regulating the Poor,* for instance, we are told that older Americans got "the Social Security legislation, which covered only those aged who worked in selected occupations and industries, with even that to begin only in 1942." Thirteen pages later, Piven and Cloward restate the point, adding that "such low wage industries as agriculture and domestic service were exempted." So far, it would appear to readers unfamiliar with the system that Social Security was a niggardly concession to the old that really served only those in relatively well-paying jobs who managed to live until 1942 to collect benefits. Three sentences later, however, we learn that "the relief program that remained was the provision for the aged, the blind, the orphaned also contained in the Social Security Act of 1935," though we are assured that control for this assistance was largely delegated to state and local officials and that "these measures did not receive public attention at the time."[32] This is the first place that the authors acknowledge that a relief measure for the aged was *also* enacted in 1935 as part of the Social Security Act. Curiously, however, Piven and Cloward choose not to explain its relationship to "Social Security legislation," which they seem to equate exclusively with the retirement-insurance plan.

Yet it is precisely the interaction between the old-age insurance and assistance programs that makes the American plan different from public welfare systems elsewhere.[33] Those older people who needed immediate relief and met certain broad criteria were able to apply for assistance. Eligibility criteria and benefit levels did vary considerably — because Congress deleted a provision that would have permitted the establishment of a nationwide baseline to determine "minimum standards of decency and health" — but ultimate responsibility rested with a federal board. An elderly person could appeal to Washington if ill-treated by a state or county bureau. And the federal government's response to the economic plight of the aged did not stop here. Policy makers hoped that the old-age insurance scheme would reduce the incidence of old-age pauperism and thereby contain the future costs of maintaining an old-age assistance program. Originally, plans called for raising funds for an Old Age Reserve Account by taxing a certain proportion of an employee's salary. At first, only 60 percent of the labor force was covered, largely because officials wanted to proceed with caution. The record makes clear, however, that old-age insurance was intended to become a universal program.[34]

Indeed, after three years of operation, expanding the old-age insurance program seemed feasible economically and administratively. Since there was more money in the Old Age Reserve Account than officials had estimated there would be, benefits that initially had been scheduled to be disbursed in 1942 were scheduled for release on 1 January 1940. More workers, including employees of banks and loan associations and seamen, were covered by the system.

A far more important change, however, was the extension of benefits payable not just to wage earners at age sixty-five but also to their widows at the same age or to their dependent children under age eighteen. In order to promote the integrity of the family unit, the federal government in 1939 amended the act to establish a "survivors" program that vastly expanded the pool of potential beneficiaries. It permitted people who were related to covered wage earners to claim that they had "earned" benefits under the Social Security system. Without nullifying the concern for "equity" that had characterized the philosophy and funding mechanism behind the 1935 old-age insurance scheme, this amendment gave far greater emphasis to the need for "social adequacy" within the system as a whole.[35]

Needless to say, the foregoing interpretation sharply differs from the one presented in *Regulating the Poor*. Whereas Piven and Cloward suggest that relief programs for the aged were reduced after 1936, I contend that the 1939 amendments to Social Security, which they choose not to discuss, immediately resulted in liberalizing benefits for the aged and had the ultimate effect of ensuring that the federal government would play a pivotal role in establishing the types and amounts of support Americans could expect to receive in old age. And during the next four decades, particularly in election years, the aged received regular increases to their benefits with the public's blessing.[36] For a politician to have recommended cutbacks to the program would have been suicidal.

On the basis of available evidence, therefore, this historian doubts Piven and Cloward's contention that the Social Security Act was designed specifically to regulate the aged poor. *Regulating the Poor* fails to offer a satisfactory explanation for the origins and initial impact of Social Security because it offers a synecdochic argument: Presuming that "social control" is the pivotal element that explains the nature and dynamics of public welfare programs for the elderly in the 1930s, the authors make the crux of their thesis out of what should have been only part of their case study. Can their model be salvaged by expanding its parameters and introducing new elements? I believe so.

Despite the foregoing criticisms, a holistic approach to the formative years of Social Security that begins with the notion of "social control" is a legitimate and instructive way to deal with this important episode in American social welfare history. The primary advantage of such an approach is that it forces the investigator to establish the extent to which policy makers explicitly or implicitly designed Social Security to be an instrument that could manipulate — and, conversely, be altered by — the citizens it served. It also helps to clarify the direct, indirect, unanticipated, and unintentional ways that Social Security was envisioned and employed as a tool in regulating other dimensions of society that impinged upon, but extended beyond, the welfare arena.

Researchers, however, must overcome two major pitfalls associated with the social-control model. First, they must not permit their current ideological predilections to distort their understanding of the past. Analysts like Piven and Cloward who have studied welfare in terms of "social control" often have been tempted to attribute unseemly motives to those in charge and to portray the poor as noble but helpless victims. Such an orientation does injustice to both groups and frustrates a researcher's ability to differentiate conditions at a given time from subsequent developments. On the one hand, ascribing too much malice and forethought to those who governed often gives them too much credit for clear thinking and assumes they had more power to control events and people than was the case. On the other hand, casting the beneficiaries of relief as decent victims presumes that the poor (as well as the investigator with the advantage of hindsight) fully grasped their needs and understood how to cope with their problems, if only they had been given the chance to do so. Less generously, it presumes that they were hapless clods capable of being molded as those in power chose. Yet, insofar as today's preoccupations inform our sense of history, surely the current welfare mess alerts us to the fact that those who make policy, or try to influence those who do, perceive "reality" in wildly divergent ways and use power to different ends with varying degrees of success. Policy making and policy executing in past times were also shaped by happenstance, by a distinctive mix of personalities, ideas, and institutional constraints, as well as by shifting societal priorities. It would be an egregious mistake, however, to assume that striking parallels exist in past and present circumstances without rigorously testing such a proposition.

This point leads us to the second pitfall that needs to be surmounted — seeking as comprehensive a picture of earlier conditions as possible. This will reduce the urge to describe and explain *all* past behavior in terms of social control. To advance the proposition that public welfare is one — even the primary — means of alleviating dependency does not require an investigator to claim that social control is the only, or all-encompassing, function of relief. Social welfare programs also reflect and result from humanitarian concern for the plight of those in need.

In the case of Social Security, for example, one might turn to Franklin D. Roosevelt's 9 June 1934 message to Congress, in which he appointed the executive committee that would draft the original social security measure, to document an unmistakable commitment to protect Americans from some of the conditions that imperiled their financial well-being: "If, as our Constitution tells us, our Federal Government was established, among other things, 'to promote the general welfare,' it is our plain duty to provide for that security upon which welfare depends. . . . Hence I am looking for a sound means which I can recommend to provide at once security against several of the great disturbing factors in life — especially those which relate to unemployment and old age."[37] The President was purposely vague about legislative particulars in this passage, but he clearly believed that ensuring the "general welfare" of American workers was a national priority. Yet the beneficent sentiments expressed here raise some interesting questions. Why did no incumbent president before 1934 initiate efforts to provide unemployment insurance and protect citizens against old-age dependency? Had there been no altruistic concern for the social well-being of the unemployed and the old before this time?

To address such issues, a researcher needs to retrace the history of social benevolence. Clearly, one would review the writings and published speeches of religious figures, philanthropists, and social reformers. One should also consult public documents, including congressional hearings and debates; court decisions at the local, state, and federal levels; as well as the proceedings and annual reports of municipal and state public welfare bodies. Visual materials such as cartoons and illustrations in periodicals and newspapers, paintings, graphics, and photographs often were designed to appeal to Americans' sense of justice and thus bolstered efforts to provide relief to the poor.[38] Finally, it is important to analyze and interpret evidence left by the targets of benevolent concern: the testimony of the aged and the unemployed not only gives first-hand insights into their adverse circumstances but also reveals much about the ways these people attempted to motivate others to act.

Recommending that future researchers describe and explain the extent to which human generosity and compassion shaped the formative years of Social Security is not an arch ploy to undermine the social control model. We are not dealing with an either/or proposition. It is possible, in fact highly likely, that Americans in the 1930s were quite sympathetic and responsive to the dire predicament of the elderly and unemployed *and* that they chose to express that concern by formulating and supporting policies that were instruments of social control.[39] Furthermore, acknowledging that some supporters of a measure to benefit "the public good" were Machiavellian (or, conversely, do-gooders) does not discredit the fact that most social welfare programs result from compromises and choices — deliberate and otherwise — by people who negotiate with varying influence, obligations, and interest and who have divergent goals and constituencies in mind. It is the task of the researcher, however, to gather all the pertinent facts, validate their accuracy, and then assess their significance.

As the preceding suggests, there is much to do before a truly satisfying interpretation of the origins of the Social Security Act as an instrument of social control *and* social welfare can be written. It will entail more basic research in twentieth-century social and cultural as well as political and economic history. We need to learn about the actual and perceived dimensions of poverty in the 1930s. We must investigate the process as well as the specific outcomes of policy making, especially insofar as they were affected by the prevailing structure of politics as well as by official and popular attitudes on social issues and governmental responsibilities. We have to explore the economics of welfare, paying attention not only to debates between laissez-faire advocates and Keynesian enthusiasts but also to the ways that policy influentials reconciled national priorities with fiscal exigencies. Once we have accomplished all this, we must attempt to put the pieces together, but not so deftly that we leave no room in our interpretation for discrepancies between theory and evidence. In addition, those who want their studies to have an impact on current discussions about the future of Social Security will be required to learn enough about modeling and program evaluation — topics rarely covered in history graduate seminars — to enable them to engage in the public policy process.[40] Although the task seems awesome, the need for such an undertaking cannot be exaggerated.

It is indisputable that Social Security has become a lively political issue in recent years, and it seems likely that it will remain so. The era in which the system enjoyed extraordinary popular support and in which politicians overwhelmingly voted in favor of increased benefits has ended. Social Security always had its critics, but the debate today is more intense and widespread as doubts mount about the system's current and future solvency. In the 1970s, policy makers tinkered with the system in a piecemeal and sometimes shortsighted manner. Experts predict that, in the 1980s, participation in policy making for Social Security will be broadened, and fundamental reforms will become all the more necessary to deal with short-term crises and long-range issues.[41]

Historians, who rarely have contributed more than impressive-sounding references in someone else's analysis, must join the debate because they have much to offer. Those who have studied the historical record are in an ideal position to suggest when past policy situations appear to be pertinent to contemporary conditions *and* when they are not. The past, after all, is not invariably an appropriate guide to the present; sometimes the most important lesson we can learn from the past is that we have nothing more to learn. Historians, however, can assist in other ways. For instance, they can help policy makers determine whether a particular phenomenon should or should not be viewed as a social problem.[42] Because they have been trained to view time as an independent variable, historians can help distinguish between perennial conflicts and more ephemeral issues, thereby offering a fresh perspective on whether discontinuities in trend lines reflect temporary, possibly self-correcting, fluctuations or whether they presage major new directions in policy needs and functions. By showing how beliefs affect policy choices and by reaffirming the diversity and inherent tensions with America's value systems, scholars can ensure that elements that should count in any policy analysis are not ignored merely because they resist quantifiable manipulation.

I do not mean to suggest, of course, that every historian must perform all these tasks. Nor do I presume that *only* historians can accomplish such chores. But I do think that case studies and macro-studies that incorporate proper historical perspective — sadly lacking in the Piven and Cloward study — ultimately will suggest better ways to formulate sound policies to ensure that Social Security's formative years were not also its best years.

NOTES

1. Frances Fox Piven and Richard A. Cloward, *Poor People's Movements: Why They Succeed, How They Fail* (New York: Pantheon, 1979), 278, 383. I wish to thank Edward T. Dunn, S.J., Peter J. Galie, Peter N. Stearns, and an anonymous reader for their criticisms of and suggestions about earlier versions of this essay.

2. Frances Fox Piven and Richard A. Cloward, *Regulating the Poor: The Functions of Public Welfare* (New York: Pantheon, 1971), xiii.

3. Michael Harrington, *The Twilight of Capitalism* (New York: Simon and Schuster, 1976), 303.

4. Peter Steinfels, "Regulating the Poor," *New York Times Book Review* (18 July 1971), 1, 26–27. Flattering statements by Gans, Merton, and Schorr appear on the back cover of the paperback edition of *Regulating the Poor* (New York: Vintage, 1972).

5. Lance Liebman, "Review of *Regulating the Poor,*" *Harvard Law Review* 85 (June 1972), 1682–91. See also the book reviews by M. Betz in *Social Forces* 50 (June 1972), 543–44, and T. Blau in *American Journal of Sociology* 17 (Jan. 1972), 108–9. The most devastating attack was made by Eugene Durman, "Have the Poor Been Regulated? Toward a Multivariate Understanding of Welfare Growth," *Social Science Review* 47 (Sept. 1973), 339–59. Piven and Cloward pugnaciously challenged Durman's critique in "Reaffirming the Regulation of the Poor." *Social Service Review* 18 (June 1974), 147–69.

6. Elliott Krause's *Power and Illness: The Political Sociology of Health and Medical Care* (New York: Elsevier, 1977) and Michael Parenti's *Democracy for the Few* (2d ed., New York: St. Martin's Press, 1977), for example, approvingly cite Piven and Cloward's views on the origins of Social Security.

7. William A. Muraskin, "The Social-Control Theory in American History: A Critique," *Journal of Social History* 9 (Summer 1976), 559–70; Raymond A. Mohl, "Mainstream Social Welfare History and Its Problems," *Reviews in American History* 7 (Dec. 1979), 469–77.

8. Piven and Cloward, *Regulating the Poor,* 34.

9. It should be pointed out that Piven and Cloward never really demonstrate that such disturbances characterized the period. My reading of the evidence is that Americans in the depth of the Depression were stunned but not much more violent than they had been in the prosperous 1920s.

10. Piven and Cloward, *Regulating the Poor,* 88.

11. Ibid., 101.

12. Ibid.

13. Ibid., 114–16.

14. Ibid., 48.

15. Three classic studies of these developments are Robert H. Bremner, *From the Depths: The Discovery of Poverty in the United States* (New York: New York Univ. Press, 1956); Clarke Chambers, *Seedtime of Reform: American Social Service and Social Action, 1918–1933* (Minneapolis: Univ. of Minnesota Press, 1963); and Roy Lubove, *The Professional Altruist: The Emergence of Social Work as a Career, 1880–1930* (New York: Atheneum, 1969). The ideas in these works have been elaborated more recently by David J. Rothman, "The State as Parent: Social Policy in the Progressive Era," in Willard Gaylin et al., *Doing Good: The Limits of Benevolence* (New York: Pantheon, 1978); and Walter I. Trattner, *From Poor Law to Welfare State* (2d ed., New York: Free Press, 1979).

16. See, for instance, Judith G. Cetina's "A History of Veterans' Homes in the United States" (Ph.D. diss., Case Western Reserve University, 1977), and Edward Berkowitz and Kim McQuaid, *Creating the Welfare State* (New York: Praeger Publishers, 1980).

17. Barry Karl, *Executive Reorganization and Reform in the New Deal* (Cambridge, Mass.: Harvard Univ. Press, 1963).

18. Piven and Cloward, *Regulating the Poor,* 101.

19. W. Andrew Achenbaum, *Old Age in the New Land: The American Experience since 1790* (Baltimore: Johns Hopkins Univ. Press, 1978), 123, 132.

20. Piven and Cloward, *Regulating the Poor,* 88–89.

21. Ibid., 104. The list of dissident groups appears on p. 88.

22. Ibid., 89–93.

23. See, for example, Daniel Nelson, *Unemployment Insurance: The American Experience, 1915–1935* (Madison: Univ. of Wisconsin Press, 1969), and John A. Garraty, *Unemployment in History: Economic Thought and Public Policy* (New York: Harper and Row, 1978), chaps. 9–10.

24. Piven and Cloward, *Regulating the Poor,* 100. Abraham Holtzman, *The Townsend Movement* (New York: Bookman Associates, 1963), 87.

25. Richard I. Neuberger and Kelley Loe, *An Army of the Aged* (Caldwell, Idaho: Claxton, 1936), 50–52, 204–6; Jackson K. Putnam, *Old-Age Politics in California* (Stanford: Stanford Univ. Press, 1971), 56–57.

26. Arthur J. Altmeyer, *The Formative Years of Social Security* (Madison: Univ. of Wisconsin Press, 1968), 9–10; Henry J. Pratt, *The Gray Lobby* (Chicago: Univ. of Chicago Press, 1976), 23, 225.

27. Louis Leotta, "Abraham Epstein and the Movement for Old Age Security," *Labor History* 16 (Summer 1975), 359–78.

28. Roy Lubove, *The Struggle for Social Security, 1900–1935* (Cambridge, Mass.: Harvard Univ. Press, 1968), 143.

29. Piven and Cloward, *Regulating the Poor,* 9.

30. James MacGreagor Burns, *Leadership* (New York: Harper and Row, 1978), 406–7.

31. Achenbaum, *Old Age,* 131–34; David Hackett Fischer, *Growing Old in America* (New York: Oxford Univ. Press, 1978), 182–85.

32. Piven and Cloward, *Regulating the Poor,* 114.

33. Arnold Heidenheimer, Hugh Heclo, and C. T. Adams, *Comparative Public Policy: The Politics of Social Choice in Europe and America* (New York: St. Martin's Press, 1975), 192–27.

34. Charles McKinley and Robert W. Frase, *Launching Social Security: A Capture-and-Record Account, 1935–1937* (Madison: Univ. of Wisconsin Press, 1970). One commentator on an earlier draft of this essay suggested that forced old-age-insurance contributions constituted a way to "control" workers, rather than just the elderly. This is one way to interpret the evidence. Indeed, William Graebner elaborates such a thesis in *A History of Retirement* (New Haven: Yale Univ. Press, 1980). I am disinclined to describe the tax as an element of social control, because it would then force us to describe any rule or regulation in a comparable manner. That, in my opinion, would so stretch the meaning of "social control" as to vitiate its analytic value. For an extended statement of this position, see W. Andrew Achenbaum, *Shades of Gray: Old Age, American Values, and Federal Policies since 1920* (Boston: Little, Brown, 1983).

35. J. Douglas Brown, *An American Philosophy of Social Security* (Princeton: Princeton Univ. Press, 1968).

36. Edward R. Tufte, *Political Control of the Economy* (Princeton: Princeton Univ. Press, 1978), 29–36, 52–54.

37. Franklin Delano Roosevelt, "Review of Legislative Accomplishments of the Administration and Congress," in U.S., Congress, House, 73d Cong., 2d sess., H. Doc. 397, 1934, 4.

38. See, for instance, W. Andrew Achenbaum and Peggy Ann Kusnerz, *Images of Old Age in America, 1790 to the Present* (Ann Arbor: Institute of Gerontology, 1978), 23, 33, 44.

39. It is worth noting that although Piven and Cloward tend to discount the importance of humanitarianism in their interpretation, they do not summarily dismiss it. Indeed, they quite deftly respond to both liberal and conservative criticisms of their thesis on this point. See Piven and Cloward, "Reaffirming the Regulation of the Poor," 147–49, 156. Presumably, they would have accorded "benevolence" more prominence in their analysis if they had concluded that the "facts" warranted it.

40. James McCurley III, "The Historian's Role in the Making of Public Policy," *Social Science History* 3 (Winter 1979), 202–8. For a succinct agenda for the next stage in social welfare history, see Gerald N. Grob, "Reflections on the History of Social Policy in America," *Reviews in American History* 7 (Sept. 1979), 293–307.

41. Martha Derthick, *Policymaking for Social Security* (Washington, D.C.: Brookings Institution, 1979).

42. Charles E. Lindblom and David K. Cohen, *Usable Knowledge* (New Haven: Yale Univ. Press, 1979), 50; Ernest R. May, *"Lessons" of the Past* (New York: Oxford Univ. Press, 1973).

SOCIAL CONTROL AND HISTORICAL EXPLANATION
Historians View the Piven and Cloward Thesis

JAMES LEIBY

University of California, Berkeley

In the program that was the origin of this book, I was the commen-tator. My colleagues had a definite job: Professor Trattner asked them to test the generality of the Piven and Cloward thesis by applying it to particular historical episodes that they were studying. My job was undefined. I supposed that it was partly to reflect upon the his-toriographical or philosophical character of the thesis and its appli-cation, and partly to review the subject and the presentations from that perspective. Accordingly, I began by distinguishing historical explanations of events from those proposed by social scientists; I then reviewed the history and current significance of the idea of social control, which is central to the thesis, and I concluded with com-ments on my colleagues' presentations and the Piven and Cloward thesis itself. Below are my revised comments.

My starting point is that I am a professional historian, a specialist in the social and intellectual history of the United States. For more than twenty years I have studied and taught the history of social wel-fare, most of the time as a professor in the School of Social Welfare, University of California, Berkeley. My faculty colleagues represent many social science disciplines. My students have been interested mostly in professional careers. I believe (1) that a proper historical explanation of events is different from a social science explanation and (2) that the people who founded and tried to improve America's social welfare institutions generally acted in public-spirited and rational ways ("public-spirited" does not imply that they were en-thusiasts, idealists, or altruists, or "rational" that their ideas were correct). As I understand Piven and Cloward, they reject both prop-ositions. They believe (1) that historical events, at least those that they consider in *Regulating the Poor,* are evidence for and illustrations of law-like generalizations, and (2) that the purpose of much philanthropic "reform" was to protect selfish class interests.

Discussions of the logic of explanation are likely to be tedious, fit only for methods courses, so it is occasion for neither surprise nor blame that Piven and Cloward do not venture one. (Neither do the essayists in this book, nor I in my own historical publications.) Piven is a political scientist and Cloward a sociologist; they evidently share a world of logical discourse, and I suppose that it did not occur to them that they might be addressing historians who would take exception, not to their facts or even their conclusions, but to the way they went about explaining events. In fact, I do not recall any reviews of their book that raised this point, although some criticisms of their argument implied it. On the other hand, historians, such as those in this volume, who also share an idea of explanation, do not ordinarily make it explicit for the benefit of social scientists who read their publications. I must acknowledge that several schools of historians disagree with my distinction between historical thinking and social science, and I suppose that many social scientists would disagree with what I take to be the assumptions of Piven and Cloward about explanation in social science. Nevertheless, I think that there is enough agreement about what I perceive to be the difference between history and social science to make analysis worthwhile.[1]

In my view, the reasoning in *Regulating the Poor* is "positivistic," similar in its intent to reasoning in natural sciences such as physics. Natural scientists define a situation and collect facts about it, observe patterns or regularities, generalize them as laws, and conceive of a process that explains them.[2] In the case at hand, the situation under investigation is public relief, an arrangement in which officials collect money from taxpayers and use it to provide subsistence for people who are judged to need and deserve this kind of help. It is easy to see that in the past the number of people on relief increased and decreased periodically and to surmise that the officials in charge acted according to a plan by which they intended to attain some objectives. The officials were designated and their duties defined by a law — the Poor Law or a successor to it — and it is plausible that the makers of the law had a purpose and the officials were carrying it out. Therefore, to explain the course of events, historians looked for evidence about the purposes of the legislators and how officials carried them out. In general, common sense suggests that the policy of the lawmakers was that government should help people who needed and deserved help, so the number of people who got relief increased and decreased with the number of people who were needy and deserving.[3]

Piven and Cloward found this explanation, and the line of reasoning that led to it, wanting.[4] They did not dispute the evidence that historians have gathered about poor relief, or the inferences and interpretations of particular authors (the Webbs, for example).[5] They generally accepted these findings, but they went on to put a different interpretation on them. As social scientists, they believed that human actions are properly understood as constituting a social system, the elements and parts of which exhibit regular patterns; that it is possible to make law-like generalizations about them; and that it is possible to explain human actions in terms of such law-like generalizations.

In this view, public poor relief gives form to certain relationships in the social system known as capitalism. Capitalism is a system comparable with slavery and feudalism, earlier arrangements in which no one imagined public poor relief in its modern English and American forms. The emergence of public poor relief along with the emergence of capitalism was not an accidental enthusiasm of law-makers. Public poor relief had a function, a job to do in the system. It had to maintain the relation between the employer and the employed. Ordinarily, employers hired laborers because it was to their advantage to do so; but sometimes it was not, and usually there were fewer jobs than people who wanted to work. If these surplus workers were not to starve, employers would have to provide for them. Such marginal employees were likely to resent their situation and be unruly. They might make trouble for the employers, and even threaten them. Legislation for public poor relief was a device of the employers (who dominated the lawmakers) to reduce this resentment and also to maintain a host of marginal laborers who would be willing to seek employment when it became available. Hence the law-like generalization: when the marginal workers increase in number and become troublesome and threatening, officials allow the relief rolls to expand; when more jobs are available, officials cause the relief rolls to contract.[6]

In this kind of reasoning, events are explained by law-like generalizations about a putative system. The system is somehow impersonal, independent of the will and even the consciousness of individual people. What officials say about their motives, interests, and purposes does not properly explain what they do; their behavior has a social function about which they may or may not be conscious.

Relief rolls expand and contract like the volume of gas changes under various conditions of pressure and temperature in accordance with the "gas laws" of physics. The empirical questions that bring out evidence for such generalizations are not: What did these particular lawmakers say about their actions? How did they understand their situation? What assumptions did they make about it? and so forth. Instead, the appropriate questions are: Are there in fact classes of people that resemble those in the putative system? Do their relationships correspond to those in the putative system? Do events follow a course that students of the system might predict? Thereby hang these tales. Piven and Cloward reviewed a number of episodes that seemed to confirm their idea of the system and how it worked. The authors in this book present episodes in which events did not take the course that Piven and Cloward might have predicted.

Given this result, some people might say, "Well, the analysis of the system and how it works does seem correct in some cases—indeed, some important cases—but not in others. Probably it fails in those other cases because it is too simple; if it were more complicated it might explain more episodes." They might then go on to introduce complications—other variables, as social scientists say. For example, they might say that sometimes unusual events had an influence on how people responded, or that what looked like similar cycles or occasions for cycles were significantly different. An example of this sociological type of criticism is *Mass Society and the Extension of Welfare, 1960–1970,* written by Kirsten Grønbjerg in 1977. She began with a different perspective on society and social change. She did not look for the developing relations of classes under capitalism, but rather the emergence of modern or mass societies, with enlarged conceptions of citizenship and its rights. She discerned a large number of variables pertinent to this change and observed how they changed over ten years in all fifty states. The argument of Piven and Cloward that public assistance is "primarily, if not exclusively, a mechanism of social control" is, she said, "too simple-minded." It "not only does violence to the data . . . , but fails to recognize—or refuses to accept as genuine—real social facts."[7]

It is quite possible, however, to reject the notion that the law-like generalization fails because it is too simple and that what is needed is a more complicated law-like generalization. One can argue that human actions are essentially different from the events and processes studied by physicists or chemists, and that the human or social sciences are essentially different from the natural sciences. Many (but not all) historians hold this belief; I do, perhaps in an extreme form. I think that the best way, the historical way, to explain social action — that is, people acting together in some mutual relation — is the way we ordinarily explain our own acts and those of people we know well, as more or less conscious, deliberate, and voluntary responses to circumstances and contingencies. The observable regularities appear because people in social life more or less willingly follow rules that they have learned more or less well ("socialization") and that seem to them more or less right and good ("values").

Of course, individuals and groups differ in how they understand and follow the rules. They disagree and even fight over them. Contingencies and circumstances have an influence that is important and often unpredictable but, in retrospect (that is, historically), understandable. The proper emphasis, I think, is not on a law-like generalization about a system, but on the situation. It may be how one particular official deals with one particular situation, or how at some time a particular type of official deals with a particular type of situation. It may be how particular lawmakers establish a particular institution, or how a particular nation shapes a particular pattern of social welfare institutions over several centuries. The important thing, apart from ascertaining the facts of the case — a task that often is tedious, confusing, and frustrating — is to grasp how particular people understood their particular situation. Situations seem (especially at the time) to be quite indeterminant; some officials are more intelligent and courageous than others, some groups better organized and disciplined, and so forth. The course of events is different in England than in the United States, in the North than in the South, in New York than in New Jersey, and so on.

Is it possible to generalize from one state or nation to another, from one century to another? Yes, but generalization comes hard and it may not extend beyond the particular events compared. How can a critic test the validity of differing generalizations or interpretations? By considering them in relation to the evidence offered to support them. My point is, however, that the historical explanation is much more like that which a court seeks in trying a case than that which chemists or epidemiologists undertake in accounting for a regularity. Are the ruminations of social scientists of any use to historians? Yes, they are like travelers' accounts: they bring out points the natives do not notice, raise questions that do not occur to common sense, and often come up with painstaking and refined observations. Good servants, but bad masters.

From my point of view, then, the interesting thing about Piven and Cloward's book was not that it was a sociological interpretation in need of refinement or correction, but that so many people paid respectful attention to it, including some historians. Even some of my colleagues in this book, engaged in empirical studies that seem to disprove the Piven and Cloward thesis, make the point that although the conclusion is somehow wrong, the argument raises questions that are somehow right. Thus, as Professor Mohl says in his essay, although Piven and Cloward are incorrect, they raise an important question: who benefits from and whose interests are served by social welfare policy?

Piven and Cloward were not merely academics when they wrote *Regulating the Poor*; they were partisans in a good cause. Their interpretation was not a tentative scientific speculation (like Grønbjerg's), but a guide to action. As Professor Trattner observes in his introduction, their book was an example of a large body of literature in the 1960s. I shall call it "protest literature." It will take careful historical research to define that period and its spirit more clearly and to judge its significance. The literature was plainly relevant to several political movements, whose specific character, dimensions, and relations are not yet fully clear.

The idea of "social control," however, was central to many of those books of protest, including *Regulating the Poor*. Piven and Cloward did not define or discuss that term. They took it for granted, as did most others (including my colleagues in this volume). They said that poor relief (public welfare) was a social control, a sort of conspiracy that allowed employers to minimize discontent and protest and make the poor take bad jobs at low wages. They contrasted this with the older (common sense) interpretation that poor relief was a sort of philanthropy, intended to relieve, or help, the needy. This analysis informed their opinion of several proposals that were offered in the 1960s to help the poor. Some of these they approved, some they did not. In any case, they saw in the events of that decade a cycle of expansion and contraction, of placating the poor and then disciplining them. Understanding the cycle, they advocated a way to take advantage of it; they thought they saw an answer to social control.[8]

Their argument applied specifically to public assistance in its relation to the labor market. They did not discuss other features of the relief system (such as medical care or child welfare), or other kinds of philanthropy or social work. But protest literature was generally suspicious about programs and agencies that were supposed to be helpful and, as Mohl suggested, raised a question about the real beneficiaries of social welfare policy.

The importance of this question is its bearing on social justice, especially with regard to a fair — perhaps even equal — distribution of material wealth and social status. There is an old and honorable political tradition in American society that the objectives of social striving should be liberty, equality, and fraternity. From this viewpoint, it is important to observe whether, in fact, social life has been, or is, free, equal, and brotherly. These values had deep roots in ancient religious and legal traditions. People in the seventeenth, eighteenth, and nineteenth centuries combined them in various revolutionary ways, opening up many utopian and practical prospects. In some respects, however, the ideas were incompatible. Some people envisioned a caring, sharing society along religious lines; others favored a more individualistic regime based on legal rights. Some favored equality of condition, others social mobility. There were communists and anarchists, abolitionists and feminists, reformers and philanthropists of many kinds. To sort out the partisans of these causes, their constituencies, and their relationships, is a major task for historians.

In England and in the United States, one of the most important developments, I think, was a refocusing of attention in the 1890s from what, at the time, was called "pauperism," meaning *dependency,* to "poverty," meaning *relative deprivation.* Students of "poverty" advanced the discussion of equality in many ways. They brought out facts about the distribution of wealth and the condition of life in the different social classes. They pointed to impersonal and environmental causes that pushed people from poverty into pauperism. They proposed ways that the state could and should act to counter unfavorable conditions and better achieve common objectives. They formulated the idea of the welfare state: a national minimum of wellbeing available to everyone as a right of citizenship. This line of reasoning led them to advocate modern health and labor legislation, social insurance, public assistance, and other social services. Ironically, it was these programs and agencies, as they came into being over fifty years, that became the targets of suspicion in the 1960s. What Piven and Cloward did was give form and substance to that suspicion: public welfare was supposed to help, they observed, but instead it was a form of social control that merely justified poverty and actually enforced it on the poor. If you wanted society to realize the ideals of equality and fraternity, and wondered why it was failing, the suspicion was very important. If Piven and Cloward were right, they confirmed it. If not, well, try again, as Professor Mohl does in the latter part of his essay.

The suspicion that public assistance (and social welfare and philanthropy in general) had failed to achieve equality and fraternity because it served the interest of a ruling class, that it in fact was designed as a "social control" of an exploited underclass, was itself a curiosity of the 1960s. Historically, the term "social control" came into currency about the same time as the term "social welfare," in the first decade of the century, and its connotation then and for years thereafter, until perhaps the 1950s, was distinctly favorable. The first substantial work on the subject, written in 1901 by the distinguished sociologist Edward A. Ross, was *Social Control: A Survey of the Foundations of Social Order.* When Ross wrote, he had in mind the late-nineteenth-century philosophical and sociological debate over individualism, the social Darwinism of Herbert Spencer. He sounded a theme that many sociologists would later develop: the breakdown of a "natural order" in which individuals were restrained in the common interest by their ties with small face-to-face ("primary") groups. As primary groups lost influence, he thought, new types of social control (restraint in the common interest) would be necessary. "'Social welfare' is merely a synonym for the gain that comes through joint action; but it is peculiar in that it does so, for the most part, at the expense of that other welfare which is obtained through individual action."[9] He then went on to describe the usefulness of the idea of social control to sociologists and to society:

> The habit of looking upon society as an organism, and of tracing the social consequences of private actions, impresses thinkers with the enormity and turpitude of certain actions that excite, as yet, little blame. Hence, the prophet of the new social ethics strives to direct against adulteration, or jerry-building, or bank-wrecking, or combination in restraint of trade, or newspaper sensationalism, or the corrupt use of money in elections, the robust feeling that now dashes itself superfluously against wife-beating or body-snatching. Diligent and expert as he is in showing the unsuspected ways in which the social welfare suffers, the sociologist cannot but become sponsor for a multitude of new commandments and new duties.[10]

Ross concluded his book by referring to "the Strong Man at whose expense you widen your realm of order and justice":

> The Strong Man who has come to regard social control as the scheme of the many weak to bind down the few strong . . . may be brought to see it in its true light as the safeguarding of a venerable corporation, protector not alone of the labors of living men for themselves but also of the labors of bygone men for coming generations . . . — of the inventions and discoveries, the arts and sciences, the secrets of healing, and the works of delight, which he himself is free to enter into and enjoy.[11]

Later sociologists were less eloquent, but they thought of social control as the social and labor legislation of the so-called progressive years that was designed to protect the health and safety of the people against abuse by greedy or short-sighted business interests. See, for example, the proceedings of the 1917 meeting of the American Sociological Society.[12]

As a practical matter, such progressive legislation, to control what were regarded as anti-social practices of businessmen and employers, encountered strong legal resistance because it seemed to violate individual rights; it was sustained in constitutional law only by a great expansion of the "police power," a line of legal thought that produced such major works as *The Police Power, Public Power, and Constitutional Rights* (1904), by Ernst Freund, and *Social Control Through Law* (1942), by Roscoe Pound.[13]

The article "Social Control" by Helen Everett in the *Encyclopedia of the Social Sciences* (1930–1935) ventured a summary. "In its wider sense," Everett wrote, "the term . . . describes any influence exerted by society on the individual. In its narrower sense, however, it has come to mean the consciously planned guidance of economic processes," especially in the trend away from laissez-faire and toward social planning.[14] The article made cross-references to "Social Evolution," "Individualism," "Collectivism," and "Public Welfare."

The change from this originally favorable connotation of "social control" to the negative association in the protest literature of the 1960s deserves more study than it has received. It seems to have developed along two lines. One was a criticism of the widely influential "structural-functional" school of sociological analysis. Critics thought that this theory ignored the importance of social conflict and did not account very well for social change, which was often (some thought always) a consequence of conflict. Marxists, who at first held the positive view, later joined this camp. In the new view, "social control" was a tactic in the conflict; insofar as it suggested a covert or dissembling exercise of power, it expressed a conception of "hegemony" in which latter-day Marxists and other analysts of conflict found an answer to some of their own puzzles.[15] Piven and Cloward are not Marxists, but they certainly advocate conflict as the best and perhaps the only way to social change.[16]

The second path to a negative view of social welfare as social control was more indigenous and perhaps more important. It developed out of a line of sociological speculation about "social problems." One school of sociologists held that social problems were a consequence of poverty, poverty was a consequence of exploitation, and exploitation was the objective of class conflict. Most sociologists sought other comprehending ideas, however. Many followed Charles H. Cooley and developed the idea of "social disorganization." Others stretched the metaphor that society was an organism to conceive a notion of "social pathology," or proceeded from the ideas of structure and function to that of "social dysfunction." Reflecting in the 1950's on the insights of social psychology and the sociology of Durkheim, they began to work out the concept of "deviance" and its relation to "social control."[17]

Edwin Lemert, one of the leaders in this movement, has written a plausible and critical account of it, *Human Deviance, Social Problems and Social Control* (1972). The effect of social psychology he noted, was to turn attention *from* the investigation of how people became deviant *to* how "normal" people responded to deviants and how their responses influenced behavior. In general, the response was to label and stigmatize the deviant, to shame or discredit him; this might stimulate the person to change his ways, but it was likely to reinforce or even exaggerate the behavior, to push the offender into a deviant sub-culture. So "agencies and institutions ostensibly organized for welfare, reform, rehabilitation and treatment give form and meaning to deviance and stabilize it as a secondary deviation," according to Lemert. Lemert himself wanted to refine these theories; he was displeased by the "vulgarization" of the theory and "its assimilation to popular causes" in the 1960s. He thought this vulgarization was related to the emergence of social forms sometimes described as "the 'welfare state,' the 'administrative state,' the 'garrison state,' and the 'military industrial combine,' terms which caption the powerlessness of individuals necessarily dependent on group organization to satisfy their needs" and which suggested "fundamental issues of human dignity and distributive justice." In that context, he said, the style, themes, and findings of deviance research seemed relevant to "civil libertarians, activists, and pariah groups seeking to advance their cause or convert their interests into legal rights."[18]

Whether in terms of conflict theory or of deviance theory, the idea spread in the 1960s that "social control" was essentially repressive, that the supposed beneficiaries of social welfare programs were in fact being victimized. Neither the bearers of this message nor their audiences were in a position to evaluate or qualify it by a well-informed and well-considered reflection on history. If they did look at the past, they were likely to project their vision upon it, looking for and finding retrospective evidence for their "model." I wish that I could invoke a host of well-informed, well-considered histories that said "Yes, but" or "No, but" and gave a better account of the actual course of events, but I must state that those writers who took up the theme of social welfare as social control were not much of an improvement over those who earlier had celebrated social welfare reform as progress.[19]

To summarize, the concept of social control was originally conceived by sociologists to refer to a large variety of inhibitions and restraints, especially to certain social reforms that were intended to protect the weak against the "anti-social" behavior of the strong and to affirm a collective social interest against a doctrinaire and extreme philosophy of economic and legal individualism. This conception was shared by those who opposed such "social welfare" measures (politically and in the courts), those who made the ethical and scientific case for individualism, the followers of Herbert Spencer and William Graham Sumner. A paradox to relish: the argument of the arch social Darwinist William Graham Sumner, that social welfare legislation is a form of social control and an instrument of social injustice, would find an affirmation more than a half-century later in those passionate radicals, Piven and Cloward. (Sumner thought it was bad for the successful, Piven and Cloward thought it was bad for the poor.)[20]

Turning to the Piven and Cloward thesis as an interpretation of history, it may help to point to propositions in it which, I believe, my colleagues and I would not dispute. The abstract word *capitalism* is a useful label for a lot of institutions that developed in a particular way in modern Western Europe. Capitalism was first identified in the nineteenth-century discussion of "political economy," and it was defined in the context of certain practical decisions lawmakers had to make about the regulation by government of the production and exchange of goods and services. Political economists recognized that one motive for production and exchange was some personal advantage, which they came to call *profit* (a word derived from *proficient*). They observed that production and exchange increased where lawmakers left people relatively free to seek their own economic advantage. Political economists also analyzed the process of production into factors (land, capital, and labor) and differentiated it into tasks (the division of labor). They recognized that an arrangement or bargain to the advantage or profit of one party might disadvantage or exploit the other. (The verb *to exploit* originally meant *to make use of;* it later took the connotation *to make use of in a mean or unjust way.)* They elaborated these and other abstractions into various systematic "models" that supported or rationalized various policies. Sometimes they conceived these models as parts of a more general "political sociology." Sometimes they supposed that such models might (or even had to) "explain" social change, such as the origin and tendencies of "capitalism."

Whether they approve of capitalism or not, historians agree that there was a growing network of free markets. People engaged in them could recognize different common interests based, at least in part, on their function as factors in or divisions of a process of production and exchange. These interests were often antagonistic, at least in part; regulation of these interests by public officials was always a subject of debate, if not conflict. Winners in the debate or conflict could secure or increase their economic interest. Some people benefited and others suffered much more than seemed fair or reasonable to many observers. There was much thought about the conflicts of interest and the distribution of wealth; many people thought the situation was fundamentally right and improving, others thought that there was something essentially wrong and it was getting worse. My colleagues and I would agree with Piven and Cloward that these were significant observations about the course of events.

In addition, everyone would agree that our contemporary social welfare institutions had many historical antecedents — labeled, prior to 1900, "charities and corrections" — and that insofar as these were formally organized and enduring, they usually were established and

maintained by people who enjoyed economic advantages. Public relief under the Poor Law — Piven and Cloward's specific subject —
was only one of these, but it was important, and in addition to helping people who were obviously helpless and friendless it helped people
who were ordinarily expected to support themselves by employment,
even by wretched jobs under miserable circumstances.

Furthermore, everyone would agree, I think, that these "charities,"
as they were called, and in particular public relief to people who were
employable, often were administered in a spirit that was deterrent
and even censorious. No one can doubt that the English Poor Law
reformers of 1834 and their followers in America viewed their policy
as a "deterrent" and said as plainly as possible that public relief should
be "less eligible" than self-support, so that a person would not choose
to receive public aid if he possibly could get by without it.

If these points are not in dispute, where does the disagreement
lie? If my colleagues find that the prediction that seems to follow
from the Piven and Cloward thesis is not borne out, how do they
account for the failure? It is possible to argue, as Alexander, Mohl,
and the Pumphreys do, that the cycle of events that might have been
predicted did not occur, therefore the theory is mistaken. But this
is not very satisfactory, because the theory rests in part upon empirical observations and analytical ideas that we all share, and it seemed
convincing to its authors, who may be partisan activists but who also
are serious, critical-minded scholars interested in reality and truth.
They may be mistaken, but their presentation also seemed plausible
to many well-qualified reviewers. So it is not enough to say, "We
looked for evidence and it wasn't there." My colleagues say, instead,
something like, "Here is a social situation, a cast of characters, a
sequence of events. This is what the characters did, and this is what
they said about it." The historians are dutifully cautious about stating
what was done and said. But they do not simply say, "We don't find
evidence for the cycle"; they say "This is the course of events as we
find it, and this story does not correspond to the cycle." That is,
they offer, to some extent, their own explanation. They go on to
say that in view of their explanation, the Piven and Cloward thesis
is mistaken, but they do not formulate the difference in a systematic
or general way.

In general, Alexander, the Pumphreys, and Achenbaum explain
events in terms of motives and purposes, and they discover these
by analyzing what people said about themselves and their situations.

They believe that Piven and Cloward oversimplify situations by interpreting them simply as reactions of economic classes and supposing that the purpose and motive of the dominant class is simply to secure and increase its economic advantage. The historians find that people had motives other than greed and purposes other than profit, that, indeed, greed and profit did not seem to enter much into the discussion. On the other hand, Piven and Cloward, I suppose, would point to results. They would say, "Well, in some cases, some important cases, we find this cycle: is it just a funny coincidence? Can you explain it without reference to economic classes and motives, political sociology and social change? But if you agree that these episodes are part of a pattern of social relations — a pattern that certainly is independent of any particular individuals who function in it — how does that patterning and tendency of events appear in your interpretation? You go about your research as if these events and episodes are all singular, as if they are not all obviously parts of larger patterns, and as if you did not have to consider those patterns when you thought about what so-and-so said on this or that particular occasion."

Mohl seems more respectful of the thesis. It does not apply in the case he presents, but he finds a parallel in the appearance of the charity organization society. He does not make the parallel very close, however. Piven and Cloward said that mass disorder would lead to an expansion of public relief; Mohl says there was disorder and a response, but it was in private charity rather than in public relief. Nor does Mohl link the response directly to the disorder or to a cycle of expansion and contraction. The parallel is simply that Piven and Cloward assert that the function of public relief is social control while Mohl believes that the function of the charity organization societies also was social control. He criticizes Piven and Cloward for a "single, mechanistic interpretation," but I am not sure that he has a multiple, non-mechanistic interpretation of his own in mind. I think he means that Piven and Cloward are right in thinking that social welfare programs are often or even always instruments of social control, but that social control does not necessarily follow the cycle they described; it may take some other form, such as a private charity organization society in the 1880s. Social control, yes, inevitable cycle, no.

As a professional historian, I am somewhat abashed by the sketchiness of the alternative explanations my colleagues offer. True, their assignment was to test the thesis, and they had only a few pages in which to do so. True, too, historical explanations are likely to be sketchy, because the evidence is likely to be sketchy — assorted documents here and there, partial in every sense, occasional physical survivals. Still, it is possible to put such fragments into a broad context, for we know a great deal about the state of society, the economy, thought, and politics in the periods about which they wrote, and it is possible to bring to the fragments and the context a lot of analytical questions and theoretical implications raised by our friends in the social sciences — questions about capitalism, social psychology, organizations and their administration, and the like. (The Pumphreys, who are experienced social workers and know a thing or two about administration, make interesting observations along this line.) To regard the fragments in relation to the larger context, to refract them, as it were, in the light of social science, to draw them into an apperceptive mass — these are tricks of the historian's trade. One sees continuities and connections. The sketch takes on color and depth, as if seen by stereoscope. Characters come to life. We understand their responses.

An ideal, no doubt. Still, we can try. Like my colleagues, I am not persuaded by the Piven and Cloward story of greedy ruling circles and hapless paupers bumping through their inevitable cycle, never understanding or learning. Their characters act like puppets, not real people. But I must confess that my colleagues do not present very plausible accounts either. Alexander says that Philadelphians were capitalists generally, and I suppose that the managers he talks about were investors or employers. They said they felt a duty toward and even an identification with the people they helped, but what did they think generally about class relations and social and personal responsibilities? In that complex of general impressions and ideas, what were their puzzles and their sense of direction? How did agencies of helping give form to such puzzles and directions? People in the eighteenth-century had a distinctive view of the nature and relation between "public" and "private": what were their general views about government, how was the general structure of government a likeness of those views, how did poor relief fit into that framework? Out of such considerations might come a fuller and more plausible story.

Nor can I see how Mohl's censorious visitors are much more plausible than Piven and Cloward's greedy conspirators. The people who set up and served in a charity organization society (cos) were, it appears, a small group distinguished by their social concern from the host of apathetic citizens. They professed to be interested in the poor and charitable toward them. They certainly gave their time and money to the cause. And yet they do not seem, in Mohl's account, to be very concerned or charitable. Mohl quotes the historian Blanche Coll to the effect that, because partisans of the COS thought that most paupers fell into their need because of personal failure, they favored deterrence: he supports this interpretation with a quote from Josephine Shaw Lowell. Mohl does not recognize a paradox, let alone try to explain it. Here were people of high social standing, beholden to no one. They said and thought that they were doing good in an especially far-sighted and helpful way, and in time their spirit did infuse professional social work in the United States. Yet many things they said and did seemed to some of their contemporaries, and seem to us, to be not very charitable at all, especially their advocacy of what today looks like deterrence. How could they say both (1) let's be more charitable and (2) let's deter people from accepting charity? Mohl simply chooses to believe that proponents of the COS were "uncharitable," interested not in charity but in "the real solution to poverty" — deterrence. Mohl's conclusion, however, overlooks the point that COS leaders in the 1880s were interested in *pauperism,* not *poverty.* At the very least, a professional historian should reconstruct his subjects' situation and ideas with more empathy and not rush to dismiss them with that epithet of the 1960s, *social control.*[21]

As for the Pumphreys' essay, I am not certain how their story relates to the Piven and Cloward thesis or what they mean by social control. I think that they are saying that the rapid spread of widows' pensions was a significant increase in public relief, but it was not preceded by large-scale disorder and it did not exhibit a cycle of expansion and contraction. Right. As for social control, they say "the movement substituted new, more constructive sets of social controls for the older, more punitive and destructive ones." I think they mean by this that some sorts of social controls are inherent and necessary in society; breaking up a home — separating a widow from her children because the widow had to work to support herself — was a punitive and destructive social control; asking the widow to meet strict eligibility requirements for a meager pension was a better sort of social control and a step in the right direction.

More generally, they interpret the widows' pension movement as one of a number of contemporary reforms that were somehow inspired by a change in opinion about the role of government. Nineteenth-century thought on this subject was dominated, they believe, by laissez-faire doctrine, in particular by the thought that public aid to needy people in their own homes was wrong because relief in workhouses was more of a deterrent. By contrast, widows' pensions not only repudiated that concept but also required government to take a new "constructive" role, to hold the family together rather than, as previously, allow or force it to break up. The Pumphreys say that leaders of the cos movement were spokespersons for the nineteenth-century view. This is paradoxical, because Edward Devine, whom they quote as representing the cos, also was a persuasive advocate of "preventive" policies and much progressive legislation; in fact, one of his arguments against widows' pensions was that they might forestall more significant preventive measures.[22] Nor were the charity organization societies supporters of institutional care for needy children; indeed, as the Pumphreys note, they had "demonstrated . . . positive results" of a mothers' pension "in pilot projects with selected cases." My impression is that this is an understatement, that in fact much of the case work of charity organization societies took form around broken families.

In any case, I think the Pumphreys' analysis might clarify ideas regarding the arguments over (1) institutional care vs. family care of dependent children, (2) foster care vs. care in the original home, and (3) private vs. public auspices for aid to mothers. In the nineteenth century, the main question was whether orphans should be placed in institutions or in foster homes; the concept of widows' pensions did not enter the discussion, although the need for them probably was greater at that time than later. Why? It is not plausible to answer, "Because people in the nineteenth century believed more dogmatically in laissez-faire," or "because they believed in deterrence." Moreover, there is a difference between the argument "Outdoor public relief is bad" and the argument "Deterrence is good." These notions, and "laissez-faire," were present and somehow related, and they found advocates and opponents in various individuals and groups. But what they meant or implied, how they were related, and how one line of thought gave way to another, need far more elaboration.

Professor Achenbaum's contribution differs from that of the other authors inasmuch as he reanalyzes one of the episodes Piven and Cloward themselves discuss. Specifically, he reflects on the Old Age Assistance and Old Age Insurance titles of the Social Security Act of 1935 and the addition of Survivors Insurance to the Act in 1939. He says that these programs were not designed to control the aged poor, nor did they follow the cycle of expansion and contraction on which the Piven and Cloward thesis hinges. This point is true, but not very telling, for Piven and Cloward acknowledge as much. They were thinking about the relation of poor relief to the labor market, and the aged poor were, as they say, "Largely relieved of the moral obligation to work by the pension provisions of the Social Security Act, as well as by the Old Age Assistance and Aid to the Blind Programs established under that act."[23]

On the other hand, Professor Achenbaum is forebearing in his comments on Piven and Cloward's historical method. He thinks their interpretation is important because it "offers a holistic model for studying social welfare that moves us beyond currently available frameworks." That strikes me as an odd use of *holistic,* which ordinarily alludes to the doctrine that in studying an organism the whole is something more than the sum of its parts, and the "something more" is usually conceived as a sort of mysterious spirit that animates the material constituents. In fact, he has in mind his observation that the authors "posit interrelationships between the purposes of relief and the political process, the occupational and class structure, market incentives, social order and violence, religious customs, and philosophical tenets." The idea of social control is helpful, he thinks, because it "forces the investigator to establish the extent to which policy makers explicitly or implicitly designed Social Security to be an instrument that could manipulate — and, conversely, be altered by — the citizens it served."

Well, Piven and Cloward certainly regard their history as an illustration of principles of political economy; it is, in conventional terms, an "economic interpretation." In principle, an economic interpretation is not a new "model." It is true that few histories of social welfare are economic interpretations, but that is not because Piven and Cloward thought in a "holistic" way and Robert Bremner, Clarke Chambers, Roy Lubove, and other social welfare historians did not. The questions about the Social Security Act that Achenbaum goes on to raise — good questions indeed — do not depend on any "holistic framework" but refer to what policy makers had on their minds. Those questions, as Achenbaum says, would make it more difficult for researchers' "current ideological predilections to distort their understanding of the past," and "reduce the urge to describe and explain *all* past behavior in terms of social control." This strikes me as a version of the criticism that Piven and Cloward offer a "model" that is too simple, and the challenge is to make it more complicated. I am not sure what Achenbaum means by *model,* but I think he means a sort of generalizing, perhaps even a cyclical theory, that will explain the course of events: a "model" of historical explanation would be like one of the "models" of behavior suggested by economic or sociological or psychological or political theory. I am dubious about the idea that you can "model" human behavior, let alone the course of events, influenced as it often is by all sorts of contingencies, including the weather, disease, or the like.

Social scientists want models because they want to predict. Well, let them play that game; perhaps some day their long-awaited Newton will appear. Meanwhile, when present indeterminacies and myopia have passed and the unpredictable has taken form, we historians can try to reconstruct characters and events as they really were, in place of what our ideological and theoretical predilections lead us to recall. Unlearn, yes, predict, no.

To turn from my colleagues' papers to the thesis itself, the good cause to which Piven and Cloward put their hearts and minds was the service of the welfare rights movement.[24] That movement took form in the 1960s among people on public assistance, especially blacks in large cities who received (or were eligible to receive) Aid to Families with Dependent Children. They and others joined together to assert and defend claims they could make on the bureaucracy that administered public assistance. Public welfare legislation was state law, complicated and often unclear. It allowed obscurity and discretion in its administration. The public welfare bureaucracy was ambivalent about claims on the system. It had a mission to help and many people in it wanted to help. Social workers thought the recipients needed a lot of help. The general public was less clear however. Its officials had passed the laws, and in the years after 1935 did much to clarify and increase the benefits available to the eligible. Hence the system grew ever more costly. The recipients often seemed irresponsible, if not deceitful. While most people agreed that the program should help the "truly needy," many suspected that large numbers of recipients were not truly needy, or that they could work but chose not to do so — no dead-end jobs for them. (Piven and Cloward thought the law was a device to make them take dead-end jobs.) Fathers deserted their families. Relatives did not look after their kin. Such suspicions led to a grudging and stingy administration.

The welfare rights movement took advantage of the fact that the law authorized claims that ordinarily were not made. It got people on the welfare rolls who were eligible but had not known it, or whose rightful application had been improperly denied them due to ignorance or administrative discretion. It gave voice to their interests in administration and policy. Besides, it perked them up wonderfully. To assert their right gave them dignity. So did the getting together. It was serious business — it was justice — but it also was fun: meet, march, chant, sing, disrupt the bureaucracy. Piven and Cloward loved it. They taught at the Columbia University School of Social Work. They were intellectuals and scholars, but activists as well, theorists, as it were, for the welfare rights movement. They found audiences across the nation. Good cause, impressive theory, feasible strategy: their audiences loved it.

It did not last. "Now that ghetto unrest has subsided (at least as of this writing)," they wrote in concluding *Regulating the Poor*, the "moral seems clear: a placid poor get nothing, but a turbulent poor sometimes get something."[25] Later reflection led them to the insight that the turbulence of the poor itself runs in cycles, and these cycles relate in part to practical problems in organization; a better understanding or organization would help to sustain the movement rather than frustrate it. This cycle too was illustrated by history, as indicated in their *Poor People's Movements: Why They Succeed, How They Fail* (1977). Always the cycle.

Piven and Cloward looked at the welfare rights movement and all they saw was turbulence. They looked at history and all they saw was social control. They did not see *welfare rights*. John Locke had not mentioned welfare rights, nor had Jefferson. The turbulent workers of the 1930s had not mentioned welfare rights. If they would have mentioned welfare rights, they would not have found an ambivalent bureaucracy to disrupt. How did the idea of *welfare rights* get in the picture? It appeared during the years Piven and Cloward discussed in the second part of *Regulating the Poor,* 1940–1960. But all they saw in those years was the repressive part of the cycle, capitalist conspirators enforcing work norms on the hapless poor.[26]

Curious and rather sad: they looked at the turbulence and did not see themselves and their audiences. They did see themselves as theorists of turbulence. They told their classes at the Columbia University School of Social Work and their audiences across the country about political sociology and the channeling of turbulence. They got a hearing — earned a hearing — because they were accredited scholars, professors at a graduate school of social work. Where did those theories come from, and those graduate schools of social work? Did capitalist conspirators have a hand in them? There was a clear historical line from Piven and Cloward back to those social controllers in the charity organization societies about whom Professor Mohl has such dark thoughts. When the poor were turbulent in the depression years, what were professors saying at the Columbia University School of Social Work?

Piven and Cloward looked at the welfare rights movement and saw turbulence and social control. They regarded themselves as theorists of turbulence, perhaps in a tradition of such theorists. They might have seen themselves in other traditions, seen other significant factors besides that cycle of turbulence and social control. They might have perceived a true story about real people rather than a law-like generalization about a putative system. That is how bad history blinds people.

NOTES

1. Questions about the method of inquiry and the nature of generalizations in natural science, social science, and history have occurred more to philosophers than to practicing historians or social scientists. There have been two lines of development in the twentieth century, one primarily German, among the followers of Hegel, the other among the advocates of "linguistic analysis" in recent English philosophy. H. Stuart Hughes, in *Consciousness and Society: The Reconstruction of European Social Thought, 1890–1930* (New York: Knopf, 1958), describes the first, and H.P. Rickman's *Wilhelm Dilthey, Pioneer of the Human Studies* (Berkeley: Univ. of California Press, 1979) is a clear account of a leading figure in that movement; the second is summarized in *Theories of History,* ed. Patrick Gardiner (New York: Free Press, 1959), and R.F. Atkinson, *Knowledge and Explanation in History* (Ithaca: Cornell Univ. Press, 1978).

2. This definition of *positivistic* and its implications comes from R.G. Colingwood, *The Idea of History* (Oxford: Oxford Univ. Press, 1946), 126–33. See also Hughes, *Consciousness and Society,* 36–37.

3. The history of public poor relief has been a central part of the history

of social welfare in Great Britain and the United States. Guides to the literature on England are J.D. Marshall, *The Old Poor Law, 1795–1834* (London: Macmillan, 1968), and Michael E. Rose, *The Relief of Poverty, 1834–1914* (London: Macmillan, 1972); T.H. Marshall, *Social Policy in the 20th Century* (4th ed., rev., Atlantic Highlands, N.J.: Humanities Press, 1975), is a largely historical account. I set forth my view of the American Poor Law in *A History of Social Welfare and Social Work in the United States* (New York: Columbia Univ. Press, 1978), 35–47 (with a bibliographical note, 364–67), 222–23, 260–69.

4. Francis Fox Piven and Richard A. Cloward, *Regulating the Poor: The Functions of Public Welfare* (New York: Vintage, 1972), XIII–XVI.

5. Piven and Cloward frequently cite the Webbs' great work, *English Local Government: English Poor Law History: I, The Old Poor Law, II, The Last Hundred Years* (New York: Longmans, Green, 1927–29), but they do not mention its general argument that in the nineteenth century "poor relief in a framework of repression" gave way to "poor relief in a framework of prevention." The notion that the legislative enactments of the late nineteenth and twentieth centuries, later labeled "the welfare state," were intended to prevent poverty is precisely the argument that Piven and Cloward reject. It is odd, given their knowledge of and interest in political sociology, that Piven and Cloward do not mention the valuable discussion of the nineteenth-century English Poor Law from that point of view in Reinhard Bendix, *Work and Authority in Modern Industry* (New York: Wiley, 1956).

6. *Regulating the Poor,* xiii, 4–8.

7. Kirsten Grønbjerg, *Mass Society and the Extension of Welfare, 1960–1970* (Chicago: Univ. of Chicago Press, 1977), 17.

8. Piven and Cloward, *Regulating the Poor,* 256–82, 337–38, 345–48.

9. Edward A. Ross, *Social Control: A Survey of the Foundations of Social Order* (New York: Macmillan, 1901), 418–19.

10. Ibid., 426–27.

11. Ibid., 442.

12. Scott Bedford, ed., *Social Control* (Chicago: Am. Sociological Society, 1918). There is a history of the idea in American sociology in Morris Janowitz, *The Last Half Century* (Chicago: Univ. of Chicago Press, 1978), 27–52. Janowitz professes to uphold and advance this traditional sense of the concept.

13. Ernst Freund, *The Police Power, Public Power, and Constitutional Rights* (Chicago: Univ. of Chicago Press, 1904), iii–v, 17; Roscoe Pound, *Social Control Through Law* (New Haven: Yale Univ. Press, 1942), 16.

14. Helen Everett, "Control, Social," *Encyclopedia of the Social Sciences,* 15 vols. (New York: Macmillan, 1930–35), 4: 344.

15. "Social Control," *Marxism, Communism and Western Society,* 8 vols. (New York: Herder and Herder, 1973), 8: 399–403, echoes the older positive notion of social control; statements of the new view are Joseph Femia, "Hegemony and Consciousness in the Thought of Antonia Gramsci," *Political Studies* 23 (March 1975), 29–48, and J.P. Hawley, "Antonia Gramsci's Marxism: Class, State, and Work," *Social Problems* 27 (June 1980), 584–600.

16. See their later reflections, Frances Fox Piven and Richard A. Cloward, *Poor People's Movements: Why They Succeed, How They Fail* (New York: Pantheon, 1977), xii, xiv, 36–37.

17. Edwin M. Lemert, *Human Deviance, Social Problems, and Social Control* (Englewood Cliffs, N.J.: Prentice-Hall, 1972), 8–12.

18. Ibid., 16ff.

19. Lois Banner, "Religious Benevolence as Social Control: A Critique of an Interpretation," *Journal of American History* 60 (June 1973), 23–41, reviews some of these works. William Muraskin, "The Social Control Theory in American History," *Journal of Social History* 9 (June 1976), 559–69, in fact discusses just two books, David Rothman's *Discovery of the Asylum* and Anthony Platt's *The Child Savers;* he thinks the theory has much to recommend it, but he criticizes "reductionism" in its application. See his critical review of *Regulating the Poor* in *Contemporary Sociology* 4 (Nov. 1973), 607–13.

20. Lemert observes that some sociologists of deviance who hold the notion of "secondary deviance" and labeling theory are "reminiscent of the dour philosophy of William Graham Sumner" inasmuch as they "start with a jaundiced eye on the collective effort of societies to solve problems of deviance, particularly when this work of social control is propagandized as primarily in behalf of the deviant" (*Human Deviance, Social Problems and Social Control,* 91–92). Of course there is an important difference between the belief that reformers and philanthropists are well-intentioned but misguided, and Piven and Cloward's belief that they are, with regard to poor relief at least, more or less deliberately engaged in repression.

21. For a full exposition of COS doctrine, see Charles S. Loch, *Charity and Social Life* (London: Macmillan, 1910). These views are readily available in his article on "Charity" in the *Encyclopedia Britannica* (Cambridge: Encyclopedia Britannica Co., 1911).

22. Edward Devine, "Pensions for Mothers," *American Labor Legislation Review* 3 (June 1913), 193–99.

23. Piven and Cloward, *Regulating the Poor,* xiv, 123–34. That statement is inaccurate, by the way. The aged were relieved of the moral obligation to work because they were perceived to be out of the labor market and deserving of an honorable retirement, and the "pension" referred to was conceived of as "old-age insurance" to which the beneficiaries would contribute.

24. Ibid., 320–30. They dedicated their book to "the welfare protest movement that arose in the 1960s; and to its leader, George A. Wiley."

25. Ibid., 338.

26. They explain the appearance of ideas about "welfare rights" as a result of the neighborhood legal service program of the Office of Economic Opportunity: "Lawyers know what they are paid to know," they wrote, "and until OEO funds became available very few knew anything about laws affecting the poor." Ibid., 206. But where did the ideas come from and what gave them their force with judges? Jacobus ten Broek, whose writings they cite, based his thinking on the well-known idea of equal protection of the law in administration; he was a close student of public welfare administra-

tion in California as a member of the State Board of Social Welfare, 1950–63, and its chairman from 1960 to 1963. Piven and Cloward never mention that there was a fair hearing procedure for recipients of both public assistance and social insurance and that fair hearings were intended to (and did) establish the notion of a right to help (as did the eligibility process as a whole). On the general subject, see A. Delafield Smith *The Right to Life* (Chapel Hill: Univ. of North Carolina Press, 1955).

HUMANITARIANISM IN HISTORY:

A Response to the Critics

FRANCES FOX PIVEN
*Graduate School and University Center,
City University of New York*

and

RICHARD A. CLOWARD
Columbia University

We were provoked to write *Regulating the Poor* because traditional histories of public relief struck us as insular and parochial. They consist overwhelmingly of descriptions of the intentions, the social ideas, and the ideological conflicts among relief reformers; of detailed accounts of the evolution of sundry relief policies and practices, combined with a numbing recitation of the dates and places, and of the persons associated with, various legislative, policy, and bureaucratic innovations. To be sure, none of this is extraneous to a history of relief-giving, but neither does any of it explain that history.

Public relief began to develop with the collapse of feudalism and the rise of market economies in the Western world. It was, in its own right, a new and significant institutional innovation. Indeed, we recognize in retrospect its even larger significance, for the emergence of public relief foreshadowed the emergence of the modern social welfare state itself. As such, it deserves to be made the object of theorizing. Why did this institutional innovation appear, and why did it survive to become the foundation of the income maintenance structure of the advanced social welfare state? We were doubtful that answers could be found by tracing relief developments alone. Instead, we thought it might be fruitful to examine the relationship of public relief to the emergence of the new industrial order itself.

Consequently, when we wrote *Regulating the Poor*, we tried to analyze the institution of relief-giving within a broader context of economy and polity. We specifically argued that relief institutions were developed by elites in their attempts to cope with two problems of social control inherent in the new market economies that were transforming the Western world. On the one side, the rise of the capitalist economy brought with it rapid modernization and cyclical depressions, both of which contributed to frequent episodes of catastrophic unemployment (a phenomenon unknown under feudalism). And when, as sometimes happened, the unemployed erupted in crime, rioting, and incendiarism, political elites began to replace the private, individualized practice of almsgiving which had prevailed under feudalism with a progressively more public and systematic form of aid that came to be known as outdoor relief. Elites, we inferred, gradually invented a new institutional practice to cope with a new political problem—the mass disorder sometimes associated with catastrophic unemployment.

On the other side, periods of quiescence were not without their problems of social control, either. Central among these was the enormous difficulty encountered by the new entrepreneurial class in molding an industrial proletariat—one that would endure long hours, low wages, and robot-like discipline in mines, mills, and factories, all of which were alien to an agricultural people habituated to work governed by the rhythms and vicissitudes of weather and season. As the entrepreneurial class struggled with this problem, another innovation appeared: the workhouse. When disorder subsided, elites began to terminate the giving of relief to people in their own homes, and to insist instead that relief would be available only in institutions. We therefore drew another inference: elites were experimenting with a way of coercing the destitute unemployed in agriculture and in the cottage industries to join the industrial labor force by saying, in effect, "Choose the Factory or the Workhouse!" These were the broad terms, then, in which we argued that the relief institution meshes with the larger economic and political order, variously moderating mass disorder and enforcing work norms, thus contributing to social stability.

It is indeed true, as all in this volume remark, that *Regulating the Poor* and its proposals regarding the economic and political functions of public relief were far more widely commented upon in the journals of political science, sociology, and social welfare than in the journals of history. So it was with some interest that we learned a number of social welfare historians were to present critical papers at an annual meeting of the Organization of American Historians and that this book-length publication would follow. The effort promised new and interesting insights about relief institutions, and thus the possibility of revisions (or extensions, as the case might be) of the disorder-moderating and work-maintaining functions that we thought characterized the relief institution as it emerged during the evolution of Western market societies.

But the promise of this venture has not been fulfilled. The papers published here exemplify the insular and parochial outlook of traditional social welfare histories in which the institution of relief-giving is treated as if independent of the organization of economic and political life. In contrast to *Regulating the Poor*, which represents an effort to explain relief history, the papers in this volume merely describe who did what, where, and when. Leiby admits as much in his closing commentary: "I am somewhat abashed by the sketchiness of the alternative explanations [to *Regulating the Poor*] my colleagues offer."[1] Nor does Leiby appear to have an alternative explanation.

These papers are disappointing in other ways as well. The marshalling and analysis of historical evidence is shoddy, and there are prominent instances of misinterpretation. For example, in order to discredit the relationship of mass disorder to relief expansion, several periods of history in which there was neither mass disorder nor growth in the relief rolls are baldly defined as having exhibited explosive growth. Moreover, the main arguments in *Regulating the Poor* are overstated, so that they can be more easily refuted. But perhaps the most grievous problem is the biased description of relief history itself. Evidence of the crucial role of mass protest by the underclasses in securing relief concessions from economic and political elites is simply ignored. This bias, as we shall now see, stems from the contributors' undisguised identification of the privileged and powerful as the only significant agents in the making of relief history.

We would like to turn first to the question of humanitarianism and public relief. In his introduction to this volume, Trattner declares that *Regulating the Poor* represents a challenge to the "traditional liberal account" of "humanitarianism" as the "driving force" behind the evolution of the public relief institution.[2] The same theme recurs from paper to paper. "If other writers have put too much emphasis on questions of morality," Alexander says, "Piven and Cloward come close to dismissing moral considerations entirely."[3] In this respect, there is a purpose that unites all but one of the historical essays in this volume (we exclude Mohl unless he is specifically cited); it is to reaffirm the primacy of the humanitarian motives of elites as the essential source of the rise and spread of institutionalized relief-giving.

The claim that we dismiss moral forces from history miscasts the debate. What is really at issue is the source of those moral forces. The historians represented in this volume attribute humanitarianism to reformers and to elites (who are generally one and the same; when they are not, reformers are necessarily dependent on elites for resources and legitimation). We, by contrast, come down on the side of common people—of unemployed people, for example, who from time to time tear down workhouses or storm relief offices.

More generally, we think the most important victories for political freedom and economic decency have been won through periodic struggles by ordinary people against their rulers: by the risings of slaves against masters, serfs against nobles, peasants against princes, workers against industrialists. Here is the locus of humanitarianism. It wells up out of the travails of ordinary people, and it acquires force as people resist the various forms of exploitation and oppression imposed upon them by their rulers.

None of this means that the oppressed are noble and their oppressors not. The impulse to humanitarianism does not stem from the class-distribution of moral virtue, but simply from location in the class structure itself. It stems from lowly station, from being the object of domination. Upend the hierarchy, make the underclass the overclass, and the result would likely be the same, the same oppression and exploitation. Humanitarianism thus has its roots in the aspirations of the subordinated, whoever they may be, to curb the power of their rulers.

It is also important to see that common people have been the crucial political force behind actual humanitarian achievements. Humanitarianism must be more than an impulse or an idea. The impulse acquires a transforming power only when people act to make it so— when they riot, strike, march, demonstrate, revolt. Leiby, in his closing commentary, denigrates mass movements and implies that it is the ideas of philosophers that bring freedom into being.[4] But they do not; struggles (usually bloody ones) do. Some people have always known that, just as some have always denied it. Eugene Debs knew it, and he put it plainly to the court that tried him for contempt after a strike in 1894 by his American Railway Union workers had been smashed by federal troops, state militia, and the police—at a cost of thirty-four dead. "If it were not for resistance to degrading conditions," he said, "the tendency of our whole civilization would be downward; after a while we would reach the point where there would be no resistance, and slavery would come."[5]

Leiby also makes a concerted effort to reaffirm the humanitarian role of relief-reformers by objecting to *Regulating the Poor* on epistemological grounds. Our book, he says, is objectivist, positivist, a latterday exemplification of Comptean "social physics" in which "the system is somehow impersonal, independent of the will and even the consciousness of individual people. What officials say about their motives, interests, and purposes does not properly explain what they do; their behavior performs a function in a system, a system about which they may or may not be conscious."[6] By this criticism, Leiby wishes to restore the intentions of elites, their humanitarian intentions, to the center of relief history.

We find Leiby's discussion of positivism quite confused, for the outlook he disclaims permeates his writing. On the one hand, he objects to what he characterizes as the positivistic view that "human actions are properly understood as constituting a social system, the elements and parts of which exhibit regular patterns."[7] He insists instead that "the best way, the historical way, to explain social action—that is, people acting together in some mutual relation—is the way we ordinarily explain our own acts and those of people we know well, as more or less conscious, deliberate, and voluntary responses to circumstances and contingencies."[8] On the other hand, Leiby doesn't mean "voluntary" at all, for in the next sentence he acknowledges that there are "observable regularities . . . in social life" and goes on to explain that this patterning of social action results "because people . . . more or less willingly follow rules that they have learned more or less well ('socialization') and that seem to them more or less right and good ('values')."[9] What that statement says is that people's intentions and actions are *determined* by values and socialization. It is an expression of the positivism of Parsons, following Durkheim, who posited a "sociological theorem" to the effect that society is a palpable reality constructed on a foundation of values and that the social part of human nature consists in the capacity to be molded to those values through the structures and processes of socialization. Consciousness, and the intentions flowing from it, are thus determined by a reified value consensus.

So it is not positivism to which Leiby actually objects. What he really means to say is that he belongs to a particular branch of positivism, and opposes its competitors. The vast majority of social scientists would agree that intentions are determined; they differ on the question of the determinants. In American social science, there has been a pronounced tendency to take values and socialization as the determinants; in much of European social science, by contrast, material forces — such as the Marxian "forces and relations of production" — are seen as the crucible in which consciousness is forged. In other words, Leiby is a Parsonian, not a Marxist, but he is a positivist nonetheless.

For our part, we think this much-debated issue cannot be settled in an either/or fashion, as Leiby appears to think when he describes himself as taking an "extreme" position in favor of the subjective element in history.[10] To be sure, people exhibit intentions, but those intentions are formed within a constraining institutional order that has an objective reality — whether feudal, socialist, or capitalist. In other words, we think the subjective and objective interact, at once reflecting and modifying one another. People's intentions are shaped in a social context, and people who act on their intentions also change that context.

With these clarifications made, we return to the matter of intentions in relief history. Let us put aside the classical debate as to whether it is values and intentions that determine material life or material life that determines values and intentions. Let us look at intentions in a purely descriptive way, which is what Leiby ends by doing anyway. Leiby does not explain why people have the particular intentions they do; he merely asserts that the historian or social scientist should accept uncritically the explanations that people give for the actions they take.

One immediate problem is that intentions are not always easily described. Sometimes they are confused, contradictory, half-understood. Sometimes there are discrepancies between publicly expressed intentions and private ones. The history of the development of the industrial workforce in Western countries is marked by continual expressions of concern for the souls of working people by employers, and they also gave no small amount of money to finance religious activities that would promote salvation. But these public expressions of purpose cannot be taken at face value, for those who funded such efforts at religious salvation knew as well as the rest of us that deeply pious people make docile workers.

In the areas of relief history, it is not so difficult to identify intentions, for most of the time the reformers were remarkably explicit

about them. When they set out to abolish outdoor relief, for example, they usually declared their purposes: to reduce costs, to deter
indolence. Thus in one historical period or another, we notice that
an entrepreneurial class attacks outdoor relief on the ground that
it interferes with the workings of a free labor market, or on the ground
that tax support for the unemployed draws so much money away
from private investment that the economy stagnates; at the same time,
political leaders slash funding for outdoor relief, or they abolish it
and substitute workhouses; and all the while, the overseers of the
poor declare that outdoor relief, by weakening work incentives, is
the chief source of pauperism, even of intergenerational pauperism.

So, having cited the long record of essentially similar intentions,
we made a summary statement about them. In these periods of
history, the reformers were expressly, consciously, and purposively
attempting to enforce work norms. The relief system, in short, performs an economic function. Despite the seemingly impersonal,
abstract, or what Leiby criticizes as the "law-like" language in that
sentence, it is merely a descriptive summary of the stated intentions
of particular reformers in particular countries in particular historical
periods. It is about what the powerful said were their purposes in
the management of relief, and these purposes took form within the
constraints and opportunities represented by an economic and political order called capitalism.

In fact, this dispute is not about whether people have intentions.
It is about *whose intentions matter.* By raising the issue of intentions in the way he does, Leiby is throwing sand in our eyes. Epistemological sand. His essay is an apologia for the powerful and
privileged. Were he a genuine advocate of the subjective element in
history, he would not have limited his attribution of intentions to
presidents, lawmakers, public-policy experts, lobbyists, or what he
calls "officials." He would especially not have done so in a commentary on *Regulating the Poor,* for we made much of the intentions
of the underclasses. We argued that history is not just written at the
top, but that those at the bottom sometimes scrawl out a few words,
too. We saw relief history as a dialectic of intended actions, actions
shaped by the unique imperatives originating in capitalist social structures. The imperatives differed depending on where people were located in the class structure. For those at the top, the problem was
to secure a docile labor force; for those at the bottom, it was to protect themselves against the insecurities of the market. Elites responded

to their problems with thought and action, with social ideologies and the mobilization of resources. So did the underclasses. And it was our point that relief structures have been located at the vortex of these conflicting intentions of the rulers and the ruled.

Had Leiby acknowledged that the underclasses possess the capacity for purposeful action, he would have been obliged to consider how their manifold expressions of resistance to official policies entered into and influenced the evolution of relief arrangements. Then he would have had to appraise our claim that the periodic expansion of relief was won by the poor, not conferred by the powerful.

One reason the historians represented in this volume cannot see the role of the underclasses in relief history is that they do not see conflict in history, at least not between people. Of course, they do say that there is a struggle to make the world more humane, but their characterization of that struggle lacks contending parties. They describe reformers entering the lists to do combat with faceless, impersonal conditions of adversity, such as "child labor" or "industrial accidents and disease." Thus the Pumphreys recall for us the campaigns against child labor without mentioning who profited from the employ of those children; they recall for us campaigns against industrial hazards without mentioning who profited from unsafe conditions.[11] Alexander chastizes us for "having labeled capitalism the villain of the piece."[12] Leiby even doubts that entrepreneurial acquisitiveness has anything to do with inhumanity and the struggles against it. Thus he "formulates" the views of others in this volume in what he calls "a systematic way": "they believe that Piven and Cloward oversimplify situations by holding that they simply are reactions to economic classes and that the purpose and motive of the dominant classes simply is to secure and increase its economic advantage. The historians find that people had motives other than greed and purposes other than profit, that, indeed, greed and profit did not seem to enter much into the discussion."[13]

If the ruling classes do not figure prominently in creating the inhumanities in this world, neither apparently do ordinary people figure much in remedying them. Again, the Pumphreys refer to a "varied group of reformers" who advocated that workers be paid a "living wage."[14] Can there be any doubt that laboring people were the critical group advocating a living wage? And they didn't simply advocate it, they rioted and struck for it, and sometimes died for it. Or the Pumphreys say that "industrial accidents and diseases inspired . . .

safety campaigns with notable results."[15] We thought it was mainly struggles by laboring people that won better health and safety conditions in the workplace; in fact, many laboring people are still struggling, like those coal miners with a twentieth century history of 1 million disabled and 100,000 killed in the mines of this country. All of this impersonal language to the effect that it is "accidents" or "diseases" or "hazards" that "inspired" nameless "groups of reformers" to press for remedies is a curiously opaque way of writing history, for it leaves out the actual contenders who made that history.

Our point is that the essays in this volume plainly describe a history without class conflict. How else can you explain the conclusion, central to every paper included here, that struggles by common people are irrelevant to relief expansion? In his Introduction, Trattner sums up the outlook of the volume as a whole: "all express serious doubts about Piven and Cloward's claims," and that means our central claim regarding the crucial role in social welfare history of indignation, anger, resistance, and insurgency among the unemployed.[16]

It is an odd moment to be confronted with the reassertion of an outlook on social welfare history that denies class and conflict. Even as these essays were being prepared and published, the relief system — indeed, the social welfare state as a whole — was coming under concerted attack by the Reagan administration and its big-business allies. How odd that the historians represented here are at such pains to expunge economic and political motives from relief history when their own moment in that history is so filled with the din of economic and political conflict. It is odder still that no one pauses in his essay on good-will to wonder how it could all be resulting in such bitter and pervasive ill-will. In any event, let us now turn to an examination of the evidence that presumably justifies these "serious doubts" regarding the role of class conflict in the shaping of relief history.

There are two general ways in which the relationship of class conflict to relief arrangements is discredited in this volume. On the one side, evidence is presented to show that significant periods of relief expansion have occurred *without* antecedent disorder among the unemployed. This is taken to mean that relief expansiveness reflects benevolence from above, rather than protest from below. On the other side, evidence is presented that mass disorder may be followed by intensified relief restrictiveness, *rather than by greater relief expansiveness*. This, too, is taken to mean that protest by the unemployed bears an uncertain relationship, at best, to the liberalization of relief-giving. Together, these two forms of evidence are said to justify the conclusion that mass disorder is irrelevant to relief expansion. We turn to the first of these two kinds of evidence.

The liberal account of relief-giving has been based on the premise that economic and political elites are moved by the needs of the unemployed to grant financial aid. Leiby approvingly restates that premise: "In general," he says, "common sense suggests that the policy of the lawmakers was that the government should help people who needed and deserved help, so the number of people who got relief increased with the number who were needy and deserving."[17] It was just this benign outlook that we challenged in *Regulating the Poor.* We said that it took mass unemployment *and* mass disorder to produce a significant expansion of relief-giving. Government did not respond to need alone, but to political conflict.

Although we did not say or imply that mass disorder *always* precipitates relief expansion, we certainly did say it was a necessary condition. This argument in *Regulating the Poor* would therefore be cast into serious doubt if historical evidence could be produced showing that significant periods of relief expansion have occurred without mass disorder. Two papers in this volume claim to provide that contrary evidence. One reviews old evidence, and the other presents new evidence.

The Pumphreys review the well-known history of the mothers' pension scheme developed in the early part of the twentieth century (a history, we note, to which they add very little). They say they have "chosen to examine the widows' pension movement from a standpoint Piven and Cloward chose not to consider," namely, "the process by which the new idea was incorporated into . . . the older cultural and legal system."[18] Their paper purports to be about intellectual history; it purports to be about trends in ideas regarding the appropriate types of relief-giving. In addition, it describes a small-scale change in the form of relief-giving that resulted from a given shift in ideas. By contrast, *Regulating the Poor* is about trends in the *actual* magnitude of relief-giving; it is about the large-scale expansion and the large-scale contraction of the rolls. It is thus necessary to point out that ideas, and the experimental forms of relief-giving consistent with those ideas, can change without effecting the magnitude of the relief rolls, one way or the other. The mothers' pension scheme provides just such an illustration. The Pumphreys fail to see that because they repeatedly confuse ideas with the actual volume of aid that flowed to the poor.

Thus the mothers' pension scheme is portrayed as "the first break in centuries-old patterns of provision" which came into being on an "irresistable tide of public sentiment" which took form in "a wave of . . . agitation and legislation that [swept] the country."[19] As a consequence, "an appreciable number of families over the country were enabled to maintain a semblance of normality." And then, for *Regulating the Poor,* the coup de grace: "There were no widespread protests on the part of women and children that might have induced appeasement by a new type of relief mechanism"; and "no civil disorders prompted the alacrity with which widows' pensions took hold."[20]

We quite agree that mass protest had no direct and immediate bearing on the emergence either of this "idea" or of this "new type of relief mechanism." Neither did the mothers' pension movement have anything to do with setting off a relief explosion. The rhetoric employed by the Pumphreys is enormously overblown. There was no "break in centuries-old patterns of provision"; mothers' pensions were simply outdoor relief by another name, and outdoor relief was hardly a discovery of reformers in the early-twentieth-century United States. Furthermore, there was no "irresistible tide" of reform, no "wave . . . of agitation"; there was a small group of what the Pumphreys call "vocal advocates" who promoted the scheme.[21] Finally, and of critical importance, all of this dramatic language about the ideals and dynamics of the reform process obscures the fact that few of the poor benefited. It is simply not true that "an appreciable number of families" obtained aid; practically none did. Notice that no statistics are given on the number of new recipients produced by this innovation—surely that is a significant omission. The numbers were in fact available to the Pumphreys, but to have cited them would have undermined their argument that mass relief-giving can occur without antecedent disorder. In 1921, for example, the Children's Bureau conducted a survey in which only 55,000 families were found to be receiving these pensions throughout the whole of the United States.[22] In effect, the Pumphreys fabricated this relief explosion out of rhetoric.

To put the matter another way, the mothers' pension scheme was an instance of what Murray Edelman, the political scientist, calls "symbolic politics."[23] These particiular relief reformers got the symbol of reform but not the substance. As for the poor, they got little except the opportunity to join waiting lists which, as the Pumphreys themselves tell us, eventually stretched back for years.[24] Relief history is filled with these episodes in which the reformers win and the poor lose. Indeed, when the Pumphreys occasionally restrain their proclivity for excesses of language, they themselves tell us that it was the poor who lost. In these more sober passages, they refer to the mothers' pension program as a series of "cautious experiments."[25] As to how these experiments worked out, they give these appraisals: "accomplishments fell far short of rhetoric"; the funds appropriated were "ludicrously inadequate"; consequently, "successes [were] weak and scattered."[26] It is these latter appraisals that are in keeping with the historical evidence.

We cannot understand how the Pumphreys could have confused the *idea* of reform with the *fact* of it — how they could have confused cautious experiments with episodes of large-scale relief expansion. It is not as if we had failed to discuss the dimensions of relief explosions in *Regulating the Poor*. One occurred after Roosevelt assumed office in March 1933; within eighteen months, 20 million people were admitted to the newly enacted federal emergency relief rolls. And there was a substantial difference between 1911, when the mothers' pension advocates were begging state legislatures for authorization and funding, and 1933, when the federal emergency relief rolls were swelling into the millions.[27] The obvious difference is that the reformers in the earlier period had no great tide of protest by the unemployed to give their pleadings political impact. No mass disorder, no mass relief. That is what we said, and the early history of the mothers' pension scheme is a classic case in point.

If a few tens of thousands of mother's pensioners did not compose a national relief explosion, what is to be said of Alexander's claim that an increase in the roster of an eighteenth-century Philadelphia workhouse from 380 inmates to 699 was, in his words, "dramatic," "major," "massive," and "explosive"?[28] Similarly, what is to be made of his further claim that the replacement of an almshouse with a workhouse that had a relatively larger inmate capacity "marked an expansion of the relief rolls"?[29] Considering how ridiculously small these numbers are, even for a single colonial city, Alexander's descriptive characterization of them is excessive at best. Like the Pumphreys, he has constructed relief explosions out of rhetoric. But this is only the more superficial way in which his paper is flawed.

The deeper flaw results from the premise with which he begins — that large-scale relief expansion can take place through indoor relief arrangements. That premise is absurd. It contradicts the whole of relief history. Massive relief expansion always occurs through outdoor relief systems, *never through indoor ones.* In this respect, the Pumphreys were at least analyzing the type of relief development through which a relief explosion could potentially occur (and through which one did occur in the late 1960s and early 1970s, after the mothers' pension scheme had come to be called Aid to Families with Dependent Children). But we know of only one instance in which the proportion of a population relieved in poorhouses exceeded 1 percent, and that was the period after 1830 in England, when the figure appears to have been 2 percent. Even at that, however, it was the other 7 or 8 percent of the English population remaining on the outdoor rolls in the same period that represented the authentic relief explosion.[30] Or we may recall that the federal emergency relief program, at its peak in the mid-1930s, brought 16 percent of the American population onto the relief rolls, and the AFDC rolls in the early 1970s contained 6 percent.[31]

Even being unaware of this larger historical generalization, Alexander would have stumbled upon it had he conformed with the usual statistical practice of using population proportions rather than absolute numbers to describe welfare growth. One never just compares absolute numbers, such as the numbers of workhouse inmates at two points in time. Too many other things change simultaneously, making procedures for statistical control necessary. With respect to the study of changes in the relief rolls, it is at least essential to control for population change. Had Alexander done so, his conclusions would have been the opposite of those he actually reached. Thus, in 1796, 380 inmates were relieved in the workhouse out of a population of 42,500, or 1 percent;[32] four years later, in 1800, during which time Alexander says "the explosion occurred,"[33] the figures were 699 out of 67,811, or still only 1 percent. In other words, the relief rolls and the population grew at roughly the same rate, so that everything changed even as the effect remained the same. The most that can be said for Philadelphia's negligible "relief effort" is that it remained constant relative to population change. It merely kept up. But when

Alexander interpreted these same numbers, he became confused and converted population growth from a control variable to an explanatory one, and thus reached this muddled conclusion: "Mass unemployment did not cause any outbreaks of civil disorder during these years. Why then did the explosion happen? . . . the city had experienced incredible growth, and most of that growth appears to have taken place during the last half of the 1790s. Thus the dramatic expansion of relief seems to have been caused by population increase. As a contemporary observer noted, the number of poor had 'greatly multiplied with the increased population of the State.'"[34]

Alexander reached the same muddled conclusion when he claimed that the shift from the almshouse (built in 1732) to the workhouse (built in 1767) "marked an expansion in the relief rolls, for far more people could be and were maintained in the house of employment than . . . in the old almshouse"; accordingly, "the evidence does not support the Piven and Cloward argument that expansion of the welfare rolls . . . happened because mass unemployment caused civil disorder."[35] But none of this is evidence of relief expansion. The fact that the workhouse held more inmates than the almshouse is a finding that must also be controlled for population growth over the thirty-five years from 1732 to 1767. Since Alexander gives no population figures for these particular years, let us suppose that the workhouse had twice the inmate capacity of the almshouse, and that the population of Philadelphia doubled. The result would be a constant relief effort, not an increased one. Furthermore, Alexander continually exclaims that Philadelphia's population growth was dramatic throughout the eighteenth century (a 350 percent increase from 1760 to 1800, for example),[36] so that the proportional population growth from 1732 to 1767 may have greatly exceeded the proportional growth in inmate capacity represented by the building of the workhouse. If that is so (and everything Alexander says about the way the poor were "flocking"[37] into Philadelphia during this period suggests that it is so), then the relative amount of relief-giving was falling.

It is therefore clear that Philadelphia's indoor relief effort was neither increasing nor *ever* anything but negligible. And that is precisely what the entire history of indoor relief would lead one to expect, whether in Philadelphia or anywhere. Even if the proportion of the population granted access to Philadelphia's poorhouses had increased from 1 percent to 2 percent, there would still be no comparison with outdoor relief explosions that have typically brought population proportions of 10 percent or more onto the relief rolls. Whatever he intended, Alexander's research, like that of the Pumphreys, inadvertently confirms one of the two central arguments of *Regulating the Poor*. No mass disorder, no mass relief.

Alexander's research also (and equally inadvertently) confirms the second of our two arguments. His paper is not about relief expansiveness, as he supposed; it is about relief restrictiveness, or what we call the work-maintaining function of public relief. One way reformers throughout relief history have driven the unemployed into the labor market is by substituting indoor for outdoor relief. With the one mode of relief replaced by the other, the result has *always* been the same: a sharp contraction in the numbers of people receiving relief. All of relief history confirms this generalization. Alexander would have discovered for himself the truth of this historical generalization had he made the appropriate comparisons. He should have added up the numbers of people on the outdoor relief rolls prior to the opening of the almshouse, and prior to the opening of the workhouse, and compared these figures with the numbers of people then admitted to these houses. We would be astonished to learn that a larger proportion of the unemployed received indoor relief than had previously received outdoor relief.[38]

The Philadelphia reformers would have been astonished, too. On the two separate occasions when they turned from more liberal outdoor relief arrangements to more restrictive indoor ones, they were quite clearly intent upon slashing the rolls. And they had two general motives for doing so: one was to reduce costs, and the other was to reinforce work norms. As to the first motive, the Philadelphia reformers were greatly preoccupied with the costs of outdoor relief. When they built the almshouse in 1732, it was with the intent, according to Alexander, "to lessen the costs" of the prevailing outdoor relief system, which had been established in the early colonial period.[39] When they decided to build the workhouse in 1767, Alexander tells us "the evidence shows" that the outdoor work relief system established in 1749 "had become both inadequate and outrageously expensive."[40] Now why did reformers imagine that substituting indoor relief for outdoor relief would reduce costs? The answer is obviously not that it was cheaper to maintain the same number of people in institutions rather than in their own homes, for the opposite is true.

Indoor relief was cheaper because it drastically limited the *demand* for relief by the unemployed. The poor hated those institutions, and small wonder. Those who entered were separated from family and friends; they faced unimaginable humiliation and degradation. Almshouses and workhouses were hell holes; pigsties; death traps. The mortality rates from malnutrition and epidemic fevers were staggering; few children born and raised in these institutions survived childhood. (Alexander says the two houses in Philadelphia were "ridiculously overcrowded."[41] One wonders what circumstances of ill-health and malnutrition that description conceals.) Consequently, the poor applied for admission only as a last desperate resort in the struggle against starvation. When they dared, they destroyed these abominations, denouncing them as affronts to humanity, and they sometimes got themselves killed for doing so. For example, during the month of August 1765 (just as the Philadelphia reformers were proposing to build their workhouse), the common people in England were pulling their workhouses down:

> Some thousands of rioters assembled in the neighborhood of Saxmundham in Suffolk, and destroyed the industry-house, in which the poor were employed. . . . In this riot, the military were called in, and several lost their lives before the rioters were dispersed.
> During the second week of August 1765 . . . a large crowd of people first gathered at Wickham Market, where the Directors of the Poor for Loes and Wilford Hundreds met to plan a new poorhouse; the crowd forced the Directors to sign a repudiation of their plan. For a week, the group went from workhouse to workhouse tearing the buildings down and demanding that the overseers commit themselves not to rebuild. They demanded that "the poor should be maintained as usual; that they should range at liberty and be their own masters."[42]

Reformers have always argued that outdoor relief arrangements erode the work ethic, so that relief mechanisms are needed that promote "habits of industry." But no matter how many different schemes are invented to promote habits of industry, the most successful reinforcement of work effort among the unemployed has always been achieved by limiting relief to "the offer of the House." When the Philadelphia overseers of the poor declared in 1769 that "outdoor relief should stop" in favor of the workhouse and that the unemployed poor "shall be obliged to move therein,"[43] they were acting on principles that came to be fully explicated by the English Poor Law Commissioners some sixty-five years later, in 1834. The English reformers were faced with an outdoor relief explosion that had brought more than 1 million people onto the rolls (out of a population of 9 million). Consequently, they decreed the abolition of outdoor relief and the building of workhouses, and they explained why that reform would bring down the rolls: "Into such a house none will enter voluntarily; work, confinement, and discipline will deter the indolent and vicious; and nothing but extreme necessity will induce any to accept the comfort which must be obtained by the surrender of their free agency, and the sacrifice of their accustomed habits and gratifications."[44]

Finally, we note that the progressive linking of work with relief was not limited to Philadelphia in the period described by Alexander; workhouses spread through the colonial world in the first third of the nineteenth century (in this respect, Philadelphia represented an early example of this trend). And if colonial practices were changing, that suggests that the colonial world was changing, as it surely was. Philadelphia, for example, was becoming a major center of mercantile capitalism and a port of entry for the impoverished immigrant masses. It was a time of a rising market ideology and the accompanying doctrine that unemployment and destitution have their roots in a permissive charity that destroys habits of industry. As Alexander says, the poor were beginning to be defined as morally reprehensible: dissolute, undisciplined, and in need of reform through the workhouse.[45] It was a time, in short, when the "dangerous classes" were beginning to crowd into the streets of colonial America, and onto the pages of American history. And with the generalized trend toward indoor relief in the early nineteenth century, the dangerous classes had their first great encounter with the work-maintaining function of relief reform.

To sum up so far, the arguments made in *Regulating the Poor* regarding the disorder-moderating and work-maintaining functions of public relief remain intact. If anything, the papers by the Pumphreys and by Alexander lend further credence to these arguments. The Pumphreys thought they had discovered a historical episode in which large-scale relief expansion occurred without antecedent disorder, but what they actually discovered was an episode in which there was no mass relief precisely because there was no mass disorder. As for Alexander, he made the unwarranted assumption that indoor relief systems constitute an appropriate site for the study of relief expansion, with the odd result that his paper makes a point opposite to the one he imagined. He, too, thought he had discovered episodes of large-scale relief expansion that had occurred without mass disorder, when in fact he merely rediscovered the way that the shift from outdoor to indoor relief brings into operation the restrictive or work-maintaining function of public relief. With all of this in mind, it is less than credible that Leiby, in his closing commentary, could have endorsed the conclusions of these two papers by claiming that the "cycle of events" predicted in *Regulating the Poor* "did not occur" and that therefore "the theory is mistaken."[46]

Now we would like to turn to the question of mass disorder and its effect on the public welfare system. With the burgeoning of industrial capitalism in the immediate post-Civil War era, the dangerous classes had another great encounter with relief reforms devoted to enforcing work norms. Mohl's essay recapitulates and juxtaposes two well-known features of the period: the widespread unrest and disorder among both industrial workers and the unemployed, and the extraordinary intensification of repressive relief arrangements. Mass disorder, in short, did not lead to relief expansion. Here the ostensible case against our position is not, as with the Pumphreys and Alexander, that relief expansion occurs without mass disorder; rather, it is that mass disorder does not always lead to relief expansion. Hence Mohl discredits our position as "mechanical."

It is puzzling that Mohl reached this conclusion, and that Leiby endorsed it, for we never supposed that there is an invariant relationship between mass disorder and relief expansion. We never said, "if mass disorder, then mass relief." What we did say is, "if mass relief, then mass disorder preceded." These are quite different statements; the one makes mass disorder a prerequisite, and the other makes it an adequate explanation of relief expansion. Ours was the qualified position. On the opening page of the first chapter of *Regulating the Poor,* we said that "when mass unemployment leads to outbreaks of turmoil, relief programs are ordinarily [not invariably] initiated or expanded to absorb and control enough of the unemployed to restore order"; and the summing up line at the close of the last chapter says, "The moral seems clear: a placid poor get nothing, but a turbulent poor *sometimes* get something." These are hardly mechanistic statements; we left the relationship of mass disorder to relief expansion indeterminate, conditional on the specification of further aspects of the economic and political situation obtaining at any given time in history.

If, as we said, the outcome of mass disorder is indeterminate, then a critical question is posed: When do the turbulent unemployed win, and when do they lose? When bread, and when bullets? This is the question Mohl should have been provoked to consider. Had he done so, he would have provided a revealing counterpoint to the particular category of cases we analyzed in *Regulating the Poor*. Ours were cases of successful turbulence, and his were of failed turbulence. Had he contrasted them, Mohl could have enlarged our understanding of the economic and political circumstances under which mass disorder does or does not lead to the expansion of the outdoor relief rolls.

There are a number of interesting and potentially illuminating lines of analysis that Mohl could have pursued. For example, he might have considered the similarities and differences between early-nineteenth-century England and late-nineteenth-century America. It is the differences between these countries and periods that are instructive in identifying the conditions under which the poor win or lose, but to see why that is so requires that the similarities first be remembered. Both were periods of momentous, wrenching changes produced by industrialization. In both instances the newly emerging manufacturing classes confronted the enormous problem of creating a disciplined and docile industrial labor force from a heterogeneous population of farmers, artisans, and peasants. None of these groups was acclimated to industrial work, and they resisted the backbreaking and mind-blotting drudgery of the mines, mills, and factories. These were times that required the smashing of old work habits so as to remold them, and thereby to create a proletarian class. In *Regulating the Poor*, we cited a number of authorities on these early problems in England, and their comments apply just as well to the emergence of industrialization a half-century later in the United States. Here is just one citation from the Hammonds:

> The men and women of Lancashire and Yorkshire felt of this new power [industrialism] that it was inhuman, that it disregarded all their instincts and sensibilities, that it brought into their lives an inexorable force, destroying and scattering their customs, their traditions, their freedoms, their ties of family and income. . . . To all the evils from which the domestic worker had suffered, the Industrial Revolution added discipline. . . . The workman was summoned by the factory bell; he worked under an overseer . . . ; if he broke one of a long series of minute regulations he was fined, and behind all this scheme of supervision and control there loomed the great impersonal system.[47]

Compared with their previous places and conditions of work, in short, the English common people viewed the new factory system as an abomination second only to the workhouse, and that outlook posed no small problem for the new manufacturing class. (This is why manufacturers so often arranged with the overseers of the poor to obtain quantities of children from the poorhouses, since children made for both an extremely tractable and an extremely cheap labor force, a point discussed at some length in Chapter I of *Regulating the Poor*.)

The problem of imposing effective discipline over the workforce was made all the more urgent by the precarious condition of capital itself in both periods. Competition was ferocious; it generated enormous instability, as signaled by the rapidity and extremes of the business cycle in both countries. Industrialists were like desperadoes, themselves struggling to survive by any means. To do so, they had to drive their workers; they had to get more work for lower wages from men and women just off the land who hated the new forms of labor. In other words, these were struggles in which capitalists necessarily had to mobilize all possible means of coercion and socialization, whether troops or relief reformers.

That relief reformers were mobilized in both periods is quite evident, and it is equally evident that they were mobilized to engage in an identical work-enforcing function. They denounced unemployment and poverty as products of outdoor relief and insisted that all who were motivated to work could in fact find work, even during depressions. Accordingly, they set out to abolish or slash outdoor relief: that was the intent of the reforms of 1834 in England, and of the reforms described by Mohl in the period after 1870 in the United States. In these and other ways, the reformers helped to legitimize an emerging free market ideology and to socialize the poor to industrial discipline. The object of it all was to give the poor no choice but to accept whatever employment was available at whatever wage offered. It was Polanyi who appropriately remarked of the effort to substitute indoor for outdoor relief in England after 1834 that "Psychological torture was cooly advocated and smoothly put into practice by mild philanthropists as a means of oiling the wheels of the labor mill."[48]

By contrast, Mohl neglects to say that the mild philanthropists of the late-nineteenth-century United States were, by their efforts to restrict access to outdoor relief, also acting to oil the wheels of the labor mill. He merely says that they were engaging in "social control."[49] In this fundamental respect, his paper exemplifies the insularity and parochialism that are so much in evidence throughout this volume, and in most social welfare histories. It is as if relief reformers act without reference to prevailing class interests and structures of power. Here it is appropriate to cite a comment by David Rothman, the social welfare historian: "To attach a label of social control . . . and to let the matter rest there hardly represents an advance. " It is, he insists, essential to ask, "Social control by whom? For what purposes? And why in this form rather than in another?"[50]

It is perfectly obvious why the charity organization society reformers, with their distinctively harsh outlook on pauperism, came to be so influential in the Gilded Age. They, like the capitalist class that was rapidly consolidating its power in this period, were social Darwinians. There were other perspectives represented in the larger relief community: perhaps a few of its members had read the works of Marx; others advocated the gentler principles of the utopian socialists; and many affirmed an ancient tradition of Christian charity. But the dominant class gave its support mainly to those within the relief community who endorsed Spencer's amalgam of doctrinal laissez-faire economics and Darwinian biology. Industrial leaders provided money and legitimation to those who, through educational and friendly-visiting programs, set out to persuade the underclass of the essential harmony of interests between employer and employee, to warn against the dangers of anarchism and socialism, and to expose the evils of a permissive charity. Whether in the England of 1834 or in the United States of the Gilded Age, the manufacturing classes were the key force in promoting relief policies intended to make the poor "industrious, temperate, thrifty, and self-reliant."

With these similarities identified, we turn to the differences, for they bring us directly to the question of why the poor sometimes win, and sometimes lose. In the England of 1834, a turbulent poor delayed the implementation of coercive indoor relief arrangements for at least several decades. Ten years after the Poor Law Commissioners ordered the dismantling of outdoor relief, for example, only 215,000 persons were in workhouses, and 1,255,000 persons remained on the outdoor rolls.[51] In the United States of the late nineteenth century, however, a turbulent poor lost, hands down. As Mohl reminds us, the charity organization society reformers succeeded in implementing many of their work-maintaining policies. Publicly funded outdoor relief programs were abolished or slashed, and the use of punitive investigatory techniques spread among many private agencies, all of which reduced access by the unemployed to relief.

This large difference probably cannot be explained by variations in the intensity of the manufacturing interests at stake, for in both countries the new industrial class was engaged in a bare-knuckled fight for capital accumulation. We suspect that the explanation (and this is a matter for further investigation) might be found in the differing capacities of the manufacturing classes in the two countries to gain control of relief policy. The new industrialists faced little opposition in the United States after the Civil War. Of critical importance, there was no landed class, with its roots in feudalism, from which control of relief had to be wrested. In this respect, English capital had a more difficult time of it, and for that reason may not have so easily gotten its way with the relief system.

Here it is important to remember that the labor requirements of the English landed gentry and of the new entrepreneurial class were, in this period, quite different. For a century prior to 1834, the landed class had been stealing the common lands through parliamentary acts of enclosure, thus driving many agricultural workers into destitution. At the same time, the landed class also promoted destitution by modernizing its agricultural practices, thus greatly reducing the need for labor. Consequently, in the late eighteenth and early nineteenth centuries, the displaced agricultural poor erupted in crime, rioting, and incendiarism.[52] To cope with these disturbances among the rural unemployed, landowners in 1796 promoted an outdoor relief system ("relief in aid of wages") that produced by 1834 what the Webbs called "a pauper host of a million or so actually in receipt of relief."[53]

To the manufacturers, however, the pauper host represented a potential industrial labor supply, but it could not be driven into the factory system until it was driven out of the outdoor relief system. For this reason, the new manufacturing class, once it gained access to political power through the electoral reforms of 1832, made it a first order of parliamentary business to obtain the passage of the poor-law reforms of 1834. But if this class had the power to obtain national legislative reforms, it apparently did not have the power to implement them, for the local authorities in the (primarily rural) parishes resisted, and the reforms were effectively defeated. Here, perhaps, the landed classes were obstructionist (this is the important question for investigation), for they still had to cope with the agricultural unemployed who could well have been driven to more widespread rioting and incendiarism by the summary abolition of outdoor relief. This difference in the relative power of the manufacturing classes in the two countries may thus explain why mass disorder led to the persistence of high outdoor relief rolls in the one case, and to the slashing of them in the other.

But this is not the place to engage in an extended analysis of the varying economic and political factors that might enable us to understand when the turbulent unemployed do or do not win outdoor relief concessions from their rulers. That was the task Mohl should have undertaken. Instead, he restated our qualified outlook on mass disorder in rigidly deterministic terms, summoned history to testify that she is susceptible to no such mechanistic interpretations, and left it at that.

Mohl's paper does have a certain value for this debate, however. It brings us back to a question much in contention in this volume, the question of whether or not relief expansiveness is best understood as an expression of the humanitarianism of economic and political elites. Although all of the other contributors to this volume join in claiming that government responds to what Leiby calls "the needy and the deserving,"[54] Mohl's paper directly refutes that claim. In the last third of the nineteenth century, government's main response to repetitive and severe episodes of unemployment, industrial strikes, and generalized disorder was to call up troops and to cut back relief. Moreover, Mohl reminds us that the leading relief reformers in this period assumed a posture of unvarnished hostility toward the unemployed. So far, then, the contributors to this volume have made no case for humanitarianism from above; nor, as we shall now see, are they any the more successful in discrediting humanitarianism from below.

The crucial role of struggles by common people in the making of a more humane world can be discredited by simply ignoring the evidence that points to it. Time and again, the historians in this volume refuse to see these struggles. Like other traditional social welfare historians, they thus have no warrant to evaluate the impact of popular protest on relief arrangements, one way or the other, for they never study that relationship. Instead of the painstaking gathering of data on protest — the numbers and characteristics of the people involved, the tactics employed, the modes of leadership, the grievances expressed, the alliances sometimes formed with sections of a ruling class, and the reverberations of protests on prevailing structures of power — one finds only smatterings of evidence and analysis, if any of either. There is much we are told about the way elites from time to time set about reorganizing relief arrangements, but we learn nothing about the way common people act to influence the course of relief arrangements. Not only do these historians fail to contribute to our knowledge on this score, but they ignore such evidence as has been developed by others — such as the extensive investigations of the anti-poor-law movement in England by Edsall, Rose, Driver, and Ward.[55] In other words, the angle of vision in traditional social welfare histories is so slanted that common people end by disappearing from history altogether, except as the objects of benevolent concern by elites.

Consider, for example, those militiamen of the American Revolutionary Army whom Alexander tells us rioted in the streets of Philadelphia in protest against "greedy merchant capitalists" whose price gouging "threatened to destroy the ability of the lower orders to survive." Here was disorder indeed: six or seven people were killed, and one observer remarked of the event that it all came close to "insurrection."[56] But since this disorder presumably had little impact on relief-giving, Alexander considers that it provides little evidence in support of the mass disorder–mass relief argument of *Regulating the Poor*. However, the grounds for that claim leave much to be desired.

First, we never said that any sort of protest over any sort of issue generated relief responses. We would not expect government to respond to race riots or rock concert riots with liberalized relief. To be sure, the relationship between the demands of protestors and responses by the state is often complex, but it would be foolish to advance the argument that expanded relief is the ubiquitous response by the state to just any kind of disorder.

As it happens, the government of Philadelphia did react to the rioting militiamen by distributing free flour, and that concession was more or less consistent with the grievance over high prices. It was, in the general sense of the term, a form of emergency outdoor relief. Alexander tells us this, but he is inexcusably vague, for a historian, about other facts of the incident. For example, the militiamen took the law into their own hands: "they arrested four men and paraded them through the streets."[57] What four men were these, we wonder? Just any four men? Or is it possible that it was some of those price-gouging merchants who got themselves seized and marched through the streets by the angry mob? And if four merchants were publicly humiliated and perhaps killed (Alexander does not identify those six or seven who died), what was the impact on prices? Moreover, we wonder whether public officials remained aloof from this conflict between merchants and militiamen, or did they try to intervene, cajoling or threatening the merchants in order to restrain prices and to restore order? Alexander apparently does not know the answers to these questions, but that did not deter him from concluding that "government responded rather weakly" to this particular episode of insurgency by the common people.[58]

Common people and their struggles also disappear from the essay that Achenbaum contributed to this volume dealing with the origins of the old-age pension provisions of the Social Security Act of 1935. Before discussing his outlook on history, however, we must enter a disclaimer. *Regulating the Poor* is about working people, whether employed or unemployed; it is about people in the labor force, not about those exempted from the necessity of working. Consequently, when Achenbaum asserts that "Nevertheless, Piven and Cloward contend that the classical cyclical expansion/contraction pattern affected the aged's welfare benefits, too," he is quite wrong.[59] We made no statement about social security pensions even vaguely resembling that one. Leiby also pointed this out to Achenbaum when he said that we "were thinking about the relation of poor relief to the labor market, and the aged poor were, [as we said in *Regulating the Poor*], 'largely relieved of the moral obligation to work by the pension provisions of the Social Security Act.'"[60]

For this reason, we would have passed over Achenbaum's paper without further comment except for the fact that he also refers continually to the unemployed, and to the unemployment insurance provisions of the Social Security Act. It is therefore not clear whether he means only to analyze the old-age provisions of the Act, as he says, or whether he means his analysis to apply to the other provisions as well. So we have chosen to respond to his paper, but with an emphasis on his comments regarding the unemployed, not his comments regarding the aged.

As we said, struggles by ordinary people disappear from Achenbaum's analysis. He is at great pains to argue that the events of the Great Depression are oversimplified in *Regulating the Poor*. But the complexities he introduces turn out to have no pertinence to the relationship between mass struggles by the unemployed and the yielding of mass concessions (such as emergency relief) by elites. It is as if one were to object to a mechanic's report that a disabled car has ignition trouble by arguing, "But that's too simple. What about the rusted fenders and the torn upholstery?" As we shall see, therefore, these complexities divert attention from the role of ordinary people in the making of social welfare history.

A principle set of complexities pertains to the protestors—their variegated characteristics, their variegated grievances, and their variegated demands upon government. Achenbaum's complaint is that we oversimplify by "lumping" together "militant labor groups" and "persons pressing for old-age pensions" and "coalitions of unemployed workers."[61] This is "unwarranted," he says, for "it confounds too many issues." Thus we "never really demonstrate that all dissident groups diagnosed what was wrong with America, much less that [the dissidents] prescribed what should be done next, in a complementary manner."[62]

We put aside the question of whether we did in fact lump together all dissident groups (actually, we distinguished among them quite carefully). The relevant question is, What difference did it make that these groups failed to coalesce? Had none of the groups won anything, then one might argue that fragmentation, divisiveness, and internecine warfare weakened them and enabled political and economic elites to ward off their respective challenges. But the industrial workers wanted collective bargaining rights, and got them; the aged wanted pensions, and got them; the unemployed wanted relief, jobs, and unemployment insurance, and got them. So what is the pertinence of this extensive line of criticism?

Apparently Achenbaum wants to make the following argument: Since the insurgents did not form a "united front" complete with a common definition of what was wrong and what should be done about it, that left the President, Congress, and social policy experts in something of a pickle. "Such lack of consensus," he says, "forced policy makers to make tough choices" among alternatives.[63] They had to try to divine what all those diverse insurgents were specifically disturbed about and what details of legislation would satisfy them. "Were those out of work," he asks, "primarily disturbed by *temporary* unemployment or *any* type of unemployment?" More complicated yet, if it was *temporary* unemployment that concerned them, "were they equally concerned about the plight of the unskilled factory worker, the migrant farmer, and the skilled craftsman?" On the other hand, if it was *any* type of unemployment that concerned them, "did they mention able-bodied women, blacks, and men over fifty or sixty, or did they really focus on the plight of able-bodied, young and middle-aged, white unemployed men?" In other words, Achenbaum is troubled that *Regulating the Poor* "does not entertain such questions."[64]

Quite right; we did not entertain such questions. And it is fortunate that most of the insurgents did not either (although their leaders sometimes did, and that was usually unfortunate). It was not participation in legislative drafting committees — whether devoted to framing a Federal Emergency Relief Act, or a Wagner Act, or a Social Security Act — that gave the insurgents of the 1930s their power. It was strikes, marches, and demonstrations. It was the threat they posed to economic recovery and to political stability. To cope with such threats, economic and political leaders commonly form committees, appoint insurgent leaders to them (with accompanying ceremony and publicity), and charge the committees with developing proposals for consideration by still other committees. This strategy is intended to minimize the power of the common people by co-opting their leaders, and it frequently works.[65] It was not, in short, the internal details of legislation that concerned us in *Regulating the Poor*, but why legislation in behalf of the poor comes to be enacted at all.

What sort of a world is it that emerges from Achenbaum's account? How does his portrayal differ from our portrayal after all of the complexities have been introduced? The difference is plain to see. Page by page, complexity by complexity, Achenbaum draws attention away from the world of the lower orders and toward the world of the upper ones: away from great waves of turbulence among masses of people, and toward presidents reflecting upon the appropriate timing and options for reform; away from angry crowds, looters, and picketlines, and toward a multiplicity of private and governmental committee structures; away from the crudely articulated grievances of the common people, and toward the intricate policy choices with which experts grapple; away from the emergent leadership thrust up by the eruption of mass protest, and toward the lobbyists for established organizations. Indeed, at the close of his paper, Achenbaum ends by actually omitting mass protests altogether from his inventory of the factors that need to be considered in explaining episodes of reform. Here is the inventory:

To address such issues, a researcher needs to retrace the history of social benevolence. Clearly, one would review the writings and published speeches of religious figures, philanthropists, and social reformers. One should also consult public documents, including congressional hearings and debates; court decisions at the local, state, and federal levels; as well as the proceedings and annual reports of municipal and state public welfare bodies. Visual materials such as cartoons and illustrations in periodicals and newspapers, painting, graphics, and photographs often were designed to appeal to Americans' sense of justice and thus bolstered efforts to provide relief to the poor. Finally, it is important to analyze and interpret evidence left by the targets of benevolent concern: the testimony of the aged and the unemployed not only gives first-hand insights into their adverse circumstances but also reveals much about the way these people attempted to motivate others to act.[66]

How telling the imagery in that final sentence: the "evidence left by the targets of benevolent concern"; "the testimony of the aged and the unemployed . . . about the way these people attempted to motivate others to act." We try to reconcile it with the actual struggles by workers for collective bargaining rights, by the unemployed for relief and jobs, by blacks for political rights. We try to reconcile it with the tens of thousands of strikes, sit-downs, sit-ins, riots, marches, and demonstrations, and with the tens of thousands of beatings, jailings, and killings at the hands of sheriffs, Pinkertons, militia, and federal troops. These social welfare histories are not just upper-worldly, they are other-worldly.

But these examples are not the worst. The worst denial of popular struggles is the failure by the Pumphreys to notice that it took more than a half-century for the symbolic victory of the mothers' pension movement to become a substantive victory for the poor. Furthermore, they neglect to mention that it was not a latter-day group of reformers who finally gave substance to the symbol; it was the post-war black movement and thus the sometime power of an insurgent poor. That power was effectively expressed in the ten years after 1963. It was then that great masses of women and children finally got the pensions for which a few reformers had fought unsuccessfully a half-century earlier. To be sure, a national mothers' pension framework, called Aid to Dependent Children, had been incorporated in the Social Security Act of 1935, but by the time the states got the program implemented, the political turbulence of the 1930s had receded, and with the ebbing of unrest little was done to bring many of the mothers and children who were destitute onto the ADC rolls. And this was so even though America rapidly entered one of the greatest agricultural upheavals in its history. Between 1940 and 1960, 20 million people were driven from the land, forced to migrate toward the cities where they endured one recession after another and thus intense economic suffering. The rolls rose by a mere 17 percent between 1950 and 1960, with the addition of only 400,000 people. But then, with the outbreak of the black protest movement, the rolls precipitously doubled, trebled, and finally quadrupled, adding an additional 9 million persons by the early 1970s.[67] How is it possible that the black struggle, the central political fact in mothers' pension history, could simply go unmentioned in the account given by the Pumphreys?

The only substantive reference to the great welfare explosion of the 1960s occurs in Leiby's commentary when he cites Kirsten Grønbjerg's *Mass Society and the Extension of Welfare, 1960–1970.*[68] This study attempts to refute *Regulating the Poor* by arguing that it is the evolution of mass society, not outbreaks of mass disorder, which explains the precipitous AFDC increase after 1960. Our position, Grønbjerg concludes, is "too simple-minded . . . [for it] . . . not only does violence to the data . . . , but fails to recognize—or refuses to accept as genuine—real social facts." One would have expected Leiby to be put off by this Durkheimian language, as well as by the narrowly positivistic methodology employed by Grønbjerg. Her analysis consisted of examining the relationship between the growth of mass society variables, such as urbanization and industrialization, and the growth of concepts of citizenship and rights, in this case rights to welfare. The analysis thus contains no social beings, only social forces; no struggles between concrete groups of people, only emanations from evolving social systems. By inference, we may conclude that the enactment of the civil rights legislation of 1964 and 1965 had nothing to do with the eruption of the civil rights movement in the 1950s, and that the enactment of the Wagner Act in 1935 had little or nothing to do with the century-long and bloody struggle between laboring people and industrialists.

This is not to dismiss the importance of socio-economic change, including the urbanization and industrialization associated with "mass society." But to leave it at that is to dismiss the history of real people, and of real struggles between them. Socio-economic change alters the terms of those struggles, and sometimes the outcomes, a point developed in the works of the historian Charles Tilly, who studied the relationships in various European countries among urbanization, industrialization, nation-state building, and the new capacities for mass struggle that working people gained by these large-scale transformations.[69] Of fundamental importance, Tilly calls to our attention the way urbanization and especially industrialization created new solidarities among workers, and thus greatly augmented their capacity to undertake mass mobilization. Thus if laboring people finally won the right to organize and bargain collectively in the 1930s, it was partly because economic concentration consolidated them in huge factory systems and thus gave them the power of the mass strike to wield in struggles with the industrial ruling class. Similarly, the eviction of a dispersed black (and white) agricultural workforce from the rural south after World War II was associated with urbanization, for these displaced peoples migrated toward the cities. But increased urbanization is not why they eventually got civil rights, as well as a good many other things, including welfare benefits. What urbanization did do was concentrate blacks in ghettos, enable them to construct new institutional forms (churches, unions, lodges, small business enterprises, newspapers, and so on), as well as to develop the leadership stratum required to direct these institutions, and thus to give them the infrastructure out of which to mount a mass mobilization like the civil rights movement. In these terms, large-scale socio-economic changes — such as urbanization and industrialization — are crucial to understanding how workers and blacks gained the political resources to win various categories of rights.

Moreover, a growing body of evidence is available on the way one political resource that urbanization and ghettoization made available to blacks — namely, the capacity to engage in mass rioting — contributed to the welfare explosion in the 1960s. Employing sophisticated mathematical techniques of analysis, a number of investigators — including Betz,[70] Jennings,[71] Issac and Kelly,[72] and Hicks and Swank[73] — conclude that rioting by urban blacks was the most powerful influence leading to the rise in the relief rolls after 1960.

And then there is the question of how Grønbjerg's analysis — which is limited to the period 1960–70 — might apply to past episodes of relief expansion. What is the bearing of a mass society argument, with such independent variables as urbanization and industrialization, on the relief explosion in the mainly rural areas of England in the first third of the nineteenth century? A troublesome question, and one we could have expected Leiby to ask before citing Grøn-bjerg as part of a general critique of *Regulating the Poor.* If Grøn-bjerg is right, there should have been no relief explosions prior to the latter half of the twentieth century, and that is a conclusion his-torians could simply reject out-of-hand.

We close on a contemporary note. Without mass disorder, there would have been no great relief rise in the 1960s; and without mass disorder in the 1980s, there is little hope that the AFDC system can be saved from destruction by the corporate mobilization being led by the Reagan administration. The intent of this assault is to restrict eligibility for relief so as to keep more people in the labor market despite persisting high levels of unemployment, the better to drive wages down and firm up labor discipline. And the new administra-tion is following historical precedent in another way as well, for it is attempting to reintroduce work relief by making AFDC recipients "work off" their benefits. As we said in the Epilogue of *Regulating the Poor,* "What begins as a great expansion of direct relief, and then turns to some form of work relief, ends finally with a sharp contraction of the rolls." The signs suggest that we have entered upon the work-maintaining phase of the relief cycle, that is, upon another one of those bare-knuckled struggles for increased capital accumula-tion at the expense of the living conditions of the lower classes, just as we predicted in *Regulating the Poor.*

In short, contemporary developments in American public relief policy thus far confirm the cyclical pattern described and analyzed in *Regulating the Poor.* Once the protest movements of the 1960s subsided, real benefit levels began to fall as state legislatures refused to raise grant levels despite rapid inflation in the 1970s. Nor have the relief rolls expanded in response to the recessionary unemploy-ment levels which have prevailed since the mid-1970s. The restric-tive phase of the cycle is moving forward.

Still, the success of this assault may not be entirely foreordained. Perhaps at this juncture in the evolution of capitalism and democracy, capital will not prevail. Although we do not underestimate the scale and force of the contemporary mobilization against entitlements, it is true that the political economy of the late twentieth century is not that of the nineteenth. The relationship of state to economy has been drastically altered in ways that provide powerful support for the idea that people have a right to subsistence, and particular legislative or executive actions may not be sufficient to extinguish that idea. Among other things, public relief, once the sole form of state intervention to ameliorate destitution, has come to be embedded in a general structure of income support programs for a wide range of constituencies, whether the aged, the disabled, or the unemployed. The profound changes in American society that gave rise to this broad development suggest the possibility that the cyclical giving of subsistence resources by the state has come to be replaced by a system of enduring economic entitlements. Consequently, we think it probable that a wide range of groups will resist the Reagan administration's efforts to dismantle the social welfare state, and that they are likely to prevail. We have come to believe, in short, that *Regulating the Poor* may represent a better characterization of the past than of the future (a position we set out in a recently published book, *The New Class War*).[74]

If this prediction is confirmed by events, it will be for the reason that the poor and unemployed, and other working-class groups as well, mobilize in disruptive political resistance, and for the reason that government will be vulnerable to that resistance. This is a critical moment; a great deal is at stake. The emergence of the welfare state was a momentous development in American history. It meant people could turn to government to shield them from the insecurities and hardships of an unrestrained labor market. And if the present-day mobilization against the welfare state fails, that too will be momentous. It will signify that the developments in American society that brought the welfare state into existence are also sufficient to insure its persistence.

The contributors to this volume are of no help in understanding these events, for they see no class adversaries in the making of relief policy. Seeing no adversaries, they fail to see the true "reformers" of the welfare state. They do not recognize that it has been the capacity of ordinary people to protest against degradation and destitution that has been the liberalizing influence in the history of Western relief arrangements. Unless that capacity is expressed again in response to Reagan's attack, the humanitarian achievements represented by the American social welfare state will be greatly eroded. In sum, the historians represented here have misread history, and disparaged our only allies. And that (to employ one of Leiby's favorite phrases) is what is "curious and sad."

NOTES

1. Leiby, this volume, 103.
2. Trattner, this volume, 10.
3. Alexander, this volume, 16.
4. Leiby, this volume, 109.
5. Howard Zinn, *A People's History of the United States* (New York: Harper & Row, 1980), 175.
6. Leiby, this volume, 92.
7. Ibid.
8. Ibid., 94.
9. Ibid.
10. Ibid.
11. Muriel and Ralph Pumphrey, this volume, 54.
12. Alexander, this volume, 16.
13. Leiby, this volume, 103.
14. Muriel and Ralph Pumphrey, this volume, 54.
15. Ibid., 61.
16. Trattner, this volume, 9.
17. Leiby, this volume, 91–92.
18. Muriel and Ralph Pumphrey, this volume, 52.
19. Ibid., 57, 60, 62.
20. Ibid., 62.
21. Ibid.
22. United States Children's Bureau, *Public Aid to Mothers with Dependent Children,* Children's Bureau Publication no. 162 (Washington, D.C.: G.P.O., 1928).
23. Murray Edelman, *Politics as Symbolic Action* (New Haven: Yale Univ. Press, 1971).
24. Muriel and Ralph Pumphrey, this volume, 59.
25. Ibid.
26. Ibid., 52, 57, 59, 62.
27. For a discussion of the federal emergency relief programs, see chap. 2 and 3 of *Regulating the Poor.*
28. Alexander, this volume, 21, 23.
29. Ibid., 23.
30. For the source of these figures, see *Regulating the Poor,* 35, fn. 68.
31. The relief explosions in the 1930s and 1960s are discussed in chaps. 3 and 6–10 of *Regulating the Poor.*
32. Alexander gives no population figures for 1796, only for 1790. We went ahead and used the population for 1790 as if it applied to 1796, simply because he claims that most of the population change for the decade occurred after 1796. One of the major problems in analyzing Alexander's paper is that he either fails to give figures for many of his assertions, or he gives figures for assertions that are historically irrelevant and fails to give the relevant ones.
33. Alexander, this volume, 23.
34. Ibid.

35. Ibid.
36. Ibid., 17.
37. Ibid., 23.
38. Alexander indicated that the reformers did not start shutting down outdoor relief until after the building of the workhouse. He also indicated that some outdoor relief continued to be given, owning to a conflict among two different groups of relief officials. But the point is that outdoor relief was greatly reduced with the building of the workhouse.
39. Alexander, this volume, 21.
40. Ibid., 23.
41. Ibid., 22.
42. Charles Tilly, *From Mobilization to Revolution* (Reading, Mass.: Addison-Wesley, 1978), 2–3.
43. Alexander, this volume, 24.
44. Cited in *Regulating the Poor,* 33–34.
45. Alexander, this volume, 24.
46. Leiby, this volume, 102.
47. Cited in *Regulating the Poor,* 26–27.
48. Ibid., 35, fn. 69.
49. Mohl, this volume, 42, 47.
50. David J. Rothman, "Social Control: The Uses and Abuses of the Concept in the History of Incarceration," *Rice University Studies* 67 (Winter 1981), 16.
51. See footnote 30.
52. For descriptions of these disorders in the English countryside, see J.L. Hammond and Barbara Hammond, *The Town Laborer, 1760–1832: The New Civilization* (London: Longmans, Green, 1917); E.J. Hobsbawm and George Rude, *Captain Swing* (New York: Pantheon, 1968).
53. Cited in *Regulating the Poor,* 21, fn. 37.
54. Leiby, this volume, 91–92.
55. Norman Edsall, *The Anti-Poor Law Movement* (London: Macmillan, 1971); Michael Rose, "The New Poor Law in an Industrial Area," in R. Hartwell, ed., *The Industrial Revolution* (London: Oxford Univ. Press, 1970); Cecil Driver, *Tory Radical* (London: Oxford Univ. Press, 1956); J. T. Ward, *The Factory Movement* (London: Macmillan, 1962). See also the work of Margaret Somers, "Political Structure, Proto-Industrialization, and Family Economy," in Ira Katznelson and Aristede Zolberg, eds., *Working Class Formation: Nineteenth Century Patterns in Western Europe and the United States,* forthcoming.
56. Alexander, this volume, 18.
57. Ibid.
58. Ibid.
59. Achenbaum, this volume, 73.
60. Leiby, this volume, 107.
61. Achenbaum, this volume, 76.
62. Ibid.
63. Ibid., 78.
64. Ibid., 76.

65. See Frances Fox Piven and Richard A. Cloward, *Poor People's Movements: Why They Succeed, How They Fail* (New York: Pantheon Books, 1977), for a discussion of these illusory sources of power and the consequences of their use on the political effectiveness of poor people.

66. Achenbaum, this volume, 84.

67. See *Regulating the Poor,* chaps. 6–10.

68. Leiby, this volume, 93.

69. Charles Tilly, ed., *The Formation of National States in Western Europe* (Princeton: Princeton Univ. Press, 1975).

70. Michael Betz, "Riots and Welfare: Are They Related?," *Social Problems* 21 (Winter 1974), 345–55.

71. Edward T. Jennings, "Civil Turmoil and the Growth of Welfare Rolls: A Comparative State Analysis," *Policy Studies Journal* 7 (Summer 1979), 739–45.

72. Larry Issac and William R. Kelly, "Radical Insurgency, the State, and Welfare Expansion," *American Journal of Sociology* 86, (May 1981), 1348–86.

73. Alexander Hicks and Duane Howard Swank, "Paying Off the Poor: The Piven and Cloward AFDC Caseload Thesis Revisited," Mimeo.

74. Frances Fox Piven and Richard A. Cloward, *The New Class War: Reagan's Attack on the Welfare State and Its Consequences* (New York: Pantheon, 1982).

ABOUT THE AUTHORS

W. ANDREW ACHENBAUM is assistant professor of history at Carnegie-Mellon University and assistant research scientist at the Institute of Gerontology in Ann Arbor, Michigan. In addition to contributing publications to various journals and books, he has written *Old Age in the New Land: The American Experience Since 1790* (Baltimore: Johns Hopkins Univ. Press, 1978), and *Shades of Gray: Old Age, American Values and Federal Policies Since 1920* (Boston: Little, Brown, 1982).

JOHN K. ALEXANDER is associate professor of history at the University of Cincinnati. He has published many articles in a variety of scholarly journals, chapters in numerous collected works, and one book, *Render Them Submissive: Responses to Poverty in Philadelphia, 1760–1800* (Amherst: Univ. of Massachusetts Press, 1980).

RICHARD A. CLOWARD is professor of social work at Columbia University. In addition to the numerous other works and three books he previously had co-authored with Frances F. Piven — *Regulating the Poor: The Functions of Public Welfare* (New York: Pantheon, 1971), *The Politics of Turmoil: Essays on Poverty, Race, and the Urban Crisis* (New York: Pantheon, 1974), *Poor People's Movements: Why They Succeed, How They Fail* (New York: Pantheon, 1977) — he has written *Social Perspectives on Behavior* (with Herman D. Stein, Glencoe, N.Y.: Free Press, 1958), *Delinquency and Opportunity: A Theory of Delinquent Gangs* (with Lloyd E. Ohlin, Glencoe, N.Y.: Free Press, 1960), and most recently, *The New Class War: Reagan's Attack on the Welfare State and Its Consequences* (with Frances F. Piven, New York: Pantheon, 1982).

JAMES LEIBY is professor of social welfare at the University of California–Berkeley. His many publications include three books, *Carroll Wright and Labor Reform: The Origins of Labor Statistics* (Cambridge, Mass.: Harvard Univ. Press, 1960), *Charity and Correction in New Jersey: A History of State Welfare Institutions* (New Brunswick, N.J.: Rutgers Univ. Press, 1967), and *A History of Social Welfare and Social Work in the United States* (New York: Columbia Univ. Press, 1978).

RAYMOND A. MOHL is professor of history at Florida Atlantic University and editor of the *Journal of Urban History*. He has authored, co-authored, and edited numerous works, including *Urban America in Historical Perspective* (co-edited with Neil Betten, New York: Weybright and Talley, 1970), *Poverty in New York, 1783–1825* (New York: Oxford Univ. Press, 1971), *The Urban Experience: Themes in American History* (co-authored and co-edited with James F. Richardson, Belmont, Calif.: Wadsworth, 1973), and *The Paradox of Progressive Education: The Gary Plan and Urban Schooling, 1900–1940* (co-authored with Ronald D. Cohen, Port Washington, N.Y.: Kennikat, 1979).

FRANCES F. PIVEN is professor of political science at City University of New York. She has written numerous works of all sorts in addition to the four books she co-authored with Richard A. Cloward, *Regulating the Poor: The Functions of Public Welfare* (New York: Pantheon, 1971), *The Politics of Turmoil: Essays on Poverty, Race, and the Urban Crisis* (New York: Pantheon, 1974), *Poor People's Movements: Why They Succeed, How They Fail* (New York: Pantheon, 1977), and *The New Class War: Reagan's Attack on the Welfare State and Its Consequences* (New York: Pantheon, 1982).

MURIEL W. PUMPHREY is professor of sociology at the University of Missouri–St. Louis. She has written, co-authored, and edited many publications, largely in the field of social welfare, including *The Heritage of American Social Work: Readings in Its Philosophical and Institutional Development* (co-edited with Ralph E. Pumphrey, New York: Columbia Univ. Press, 1961).

RALPH E. PUMPHREY is professor emeritus of social work at the George Warren Brown School of Social Work, Washington University, in St. Louis. In addition to co-editing *The Heritage of American-*

Social Work: Readings in Its Philosophical and Institutional Development (with Muriel E. Pumphrey, New York: Columbia Univ. Press, 1961), his works have appeared in several scholarly journals.

WALTER I. TRATTNER is professor of history at the University of Wisconsin–Milwaukee and the initiator of this volume. A former president of the Social Welfare History Group, he has authored numerous articles and three books, *Homer Folks: Pioneer in Social Welfare* (New York: Columbia Univ. Press, 1968), *Crusade for the Children: A History of the National Child Labor Committee and Child Labor Reform in America* (Chicago: Quadrangle, 1970), and *From Poor Law to Welfare State: A History of Social Welfare in America* (2d ed., rev., New York: Free Press, 1979).

SUGGESTED ADDITIONAL READING

Because all the essays in this volume are extensively documented and the works of the revisionists, and their critics, are so numerous, it seems best to provide a short bibliographical essay rather than a conventional bibliography. The following, then, is a guide to some additional reading on both *Regulating the Poor* and the social control thesis in general. It is by no means an exhaustive list; on the contrary, it is a brief selective sampling for those who wish to pursue the subject a bit further. Some of the works are cited in the footnotes to the various essays; most are not.

One of the first scholars to express reservations about *Regulating the Poor* was Gordon Rose. In "*Regulating the Poor:* An Essay Review," *Social Service Review* 45 (Dec. 1971), 393–99, he raised some objections to Piven and Cloward's assumption that capitalist regimes respond to human need only when forced to do so by disruptive mass protest. In the end, however, Rose congratulated them for undertaking a job that needed to be done, and for doing it rather well.

Far more critical was Eugene Durman, who, in an essay entitled "Have the Poor Been Regulated?: Toward a Multivariate Understanding of Welfare Growth," *Social Service Review* 47 (Sept. 1973), 339–59, argued that Piven and Cloward's attempt to explain the welfare expansion of the 1960s as merely an effort to regulate the poor was inadequate; it did not deal broadly enough with welfare as a complex social institution interacting with other social institutions and with demographic trends (an argument other, more recent students of the subject would make). The growth of the welfare rolls was an unanticipated consequence of, among other factors, an expanded pool of families eligible to receive aid and a broad movement toward social reform, according to Durman, not a result of conscious government manipulation. Piven and Cloward, however, vigorously defended themselves against those criticisms. See their

"Reaffirming the Regulation of the Poor," *Social Service Review* 48 (June 1974), 147–69.

Robert B. Albritton also tried to determine whether the liberalized social welfare policies of the 1960s, and the subsequent increase in the relief rolls, was a political response to the social disorder of the decade, and he, too, found Piven and Cloward's explanation wanting. The data, he concluded in "Social Amelioration Through Mass Insurgency? A Reexamination of the Piven and Cloward Thesis," *American Political Science Review* 73 (Dec. 1979), 1003–11, simply did not support their thesis. Albritton provided an alternative explanation, one that, in effect, maintained that the growth in the welfare rolls during the period was due mainly to amendments in the Social Security Act — amendments not occasioned by lower-class turbulence. Readers, however, again should consult Piven and Cloward's rebuttal, "Electoral Instability, Civil Disorder, and Relief Rises: A Reply to Albritton," *American Political Science Review* 73 (Dec. 1979), 1012–23.

Another critic, Michael Betz, took a slightly different approach. In a study on "Riots and Welfare: Are They Related?," *Social Problems* 21 (Winter 1974), 345–55, he found that cities in which riots occurred did indeed have budgetary increases in welfare the year following such disturbances, and nonriot cities had no such pattern. The social logic used by Piven and Cloward to explain that correlation, however, was not satisfactory to Betz. In his opinion, a variety of other explanations could have accounted for the phenomenon, including the fact that more relief was necessary in those cities because of the destruction wrought by the riots, something Piven and Cloward failed to consider.

Another scholar who argued that, whereas Piven and Cloward *may* be right, they have not definitely proved their case, is William A. Muraskin. "When we look carefully at the discussion of the post–New Deal welfare situation," he wrote in a review essay of *Regulating the Poor (Contemporary Sociology* 4 [Nov. 1975], 607–13), "we cannot definitely say [that the Piven and Cloward thesis] . . . is not provable, simply that it is not proven." Piven and Cloward's evidence is not supportive of their thesis, according to Muraskin, especially with regard to the motivations of the politicians responsible for the welfare reforms of the 1960s; either the evidence is too weak or it lends itself to a different and more plausible interpretation, Muraskin concluded.

Another critic on the same (as well as other) grounds is Joan Higgins, who, in an essay entitled "Regulating the Poor Revisited," *Journal of Social Policy* 7 (April 1978), 189–98, took the position that, although social control was an important aspect of social welfare policy, in Great Britain as well as America, there is little evidence to support the idea of conspiracy. It should not be assumed that the existence of social control is evidence of conspiracy, or, conversely, that conspiracy necessarily involves the overt use of social control, according to Higgins. While there are many other works that could be mentioned, the above are a representative sample.

Readers, however, may want to familiarize themselves with some of the other major revisionist accounts. One of the more influential is Anthony M. Platt's *The Child-Savers: The Invention of Delinquency* (Chicago: Univ. of Chicago Press, 1969). In this treatment of the evolution of the concept of juvenile delinquency and the steps leading to the creation of the juvenile court system in late-nineteenth-century America, Platt left little room for altruism. Not humanitarianism, but rather the desire of the middle classes to control lower-class children, the professional strivings of those involved with penal and correctional institutions, and especially the attempt by middle-class women to establish careers for themselves account for these developments, in the opinion of Platt.

Another important work of this genre is Paul Boyer's *Urban Masses and Moral Order in America, 1820–1920* (Cambridge, Mass.: Harvard Univ. Press, 1978), a synthesis of urban philanthropy between the Jacksonian era and the so-called affluent decade in which the author contends that an urban social-control tradition dominated social policy during the period under discussion. Throughout the century, Boyer argues, fears about industrialization, immigration, family disruption, religious change, and deepening class divisions tended to unite social thinkers, reformers, philanthropists, and others in a common effort to control the behavior of an increasingly urbanized populace.

Leading members of the business community were especially concerned about the growing disorder in nineteenth-century American cities, according to Allan S. Horlick, whose *Country Boys and Merchant Princes: The Social Control of Young Men in New York* (Lewisburg, Pa.: Bucknell Univ. Press, 1975) bears many similarities to Boyer's work. Casting around for agencies that would enable them to re-establish control of the social order that previously rested exclusively in their hands, the business elite, especially merchants, created various social institutions, particularly the YMCA, to regulate the conduct of newcomers to the city and normalize an environment that was passing out of control — and threatening their profits.

Similarly, William Graebner, in one of the most recent of the New Left or revisionist studies — *A History of Retirement: The Meaning and Function of an American Institution, 1885-1978* (New Haven: Yale Univ. Press, 1981), the first full-length work on the subject — maintained that retirement policy developed in the United States not to serve the needs of the elderly but rather those of the marketplace. Pension plans were created, and have been used, not for purposes of social justice but rather because they were seen by the corporate elite as an effective mechanism for achieving other, more important social and economic goals — the removal of older people from the labor force and a more stable social order, or, more simply stated, efficiency and social control.

There are, of course, a variety of works expressing the other, more traditional point of view. Students of child welfare, especially juvenile justice, may want to read Ellen Ryerson's *The Best-Laid Plans: America's Juvenile Court Experiment* (New York: Hill and Wang, 1978). This succinct work, which deals not only with the origin of the juvenile court and the assumptions on which it was based but with its fate as a reform idea as well, argues that the children's court was a product of the progressive era and embodied many widely held ideas; it was not created merely to fulfill the personal needs of the middle class, especially those of women searching for meaningful experiences. Further, those who created the court sincerely sought to help young offenders, and society; although they may have failed, they were not motivated, as Platt claimed, by authoritarianism, self-interest, or a desire for social control in its sinister sense.

With regard to social reform in general in the nineteenth century, especially during the ante-bellum period, readers may want to consult the following: John L. Thomas, "Romantic Reform in America, 1815-1865," *American Quarterly* 17 (Winter 1965), 656-81, in which the author argues that progressive and perfectionist, or humanitarian, impulses imbued reform efforts, not a desire for social control; Lois W. Banner, "Religious Benevolence as Social Control: A Critique of an Interpretation," *Journal of American History* 60 (June 1973), 23-41, in which the author concludes that the religious reformers had little conscious desire to control society or to resurrect an older

social order in which they were supreme. Rather, they sought to ensure the success of the American republic and the attainment of a
stable, democratic society; and M. J. Heale, "From City Fathers to
Social Critics: Humanitarianism and Government in New York,
1790–1860," *Journal of American History* 58 (June 1976), 21–41,
in which the author maintains that "civic stewardship," not social
control, was the major motivating impulse; that humanitarian activity was one of the functions that the elite adopted as a consequence
of its social position; and that to ascribe "benevolent activities solely
to the conservative temperament of an elite interested in maintaining the status quo is to view them from too narrow a perspective."

Three other full-length accounts, all on social welfare, are worthy
of note—Dorothy B. James, *Poverty, Politics, and Change* (Englewood Cliffs, N.J.: Prentice-Hall, 1972); Joe F. Feagin, *Subordinating
the Poor* (Englewood Cliffs, N.J.: Prentice-Hall, 1975); and James
Patterson, *America's Struggle Against Poverty, 1900–1980* (Cambridge, Mass.: Harvard Univ. Press, 1981). The first two works examine the welfare issue in the context of the American value system
and contend that the attitudes and beliefs of the general public, including the poor themselves, have been important determining factors in the evolution of the American welfare system. The third, an
analysis of American public policy in the twentieth century and the
latest work on the subject, takes Piven and Cloward and the other
social control advocates to task both implicitly and explicitly. The
welfare state, according to Patterson, was not shaped primarily by
the corporate elite's desire to bolster the work ethic and preserve capitalism, or by social unrest on the part of the nation's poor. Rather,
it is the product of a variety of other factors, including the good
intentions of middle-class reformers. Most important, however, in
Patterson's opinion, are economic forces, both the collapse of the
economy, which initiated the welfare state in the 1930s, and unprecedented economic growth, which prompted, and permitted, many
advances in the 1960s and early 1970s; demographic changes, especially the aging of the population, mass movements from rural to
urban areas, and a dramatic rise in the number of broken families;
and, finally, several political and institutional forces, especially the
nationalization of politics, the growing number of pressure groups
(especially among the aged), and, significantly, the bureaucratic expansion of established federal programs and agencies. The "welfare
establishment," in other words, was not the enemy, despite many

views to the contrary. Indeed, HEW was a liberal burreaucracy that continually sought to aggrandize itself, and welfare recipients often benefited from its success, according to Patterson's account.

Before concluding, several additional works should be called to the reader's attention, including William A. Muraskin's "The Social Control Theory in American History: A Critique," *Journal of Social History* 9 (Summer 1976), 559–69. While basically sympathetic to the social control interpretation, or at least to its potential, Muraskin is critical of most of the scholarship to date on the subject. In this article, ostensibly a review of Platt's book and David Rothman's *The Discovery of the Asylum* (Boston: Little, Brown, 1971), he identifies the positive qualities of the social control thesis and then critically examines the argument in an effort to point out its strengths and weaknesses. In a somewhat similar vein, David Rothman, in an article Piven and Cloward quote in their essay, "Social Control: The Uses and Abuses of the Concept in the History of Incarceration," *Rice University Studies* 67 (Winter 1981), 9–19, points out the short-comings of facilely attributing developments, and motives, to "social control." In most instances, he indicates, they are too complicated to allow for an either-or approach; it usually "is not a question of reform *or* social control, ideology *or* reality, nobility on one hand or capitalism on the other." "There is no quick fix available" in social welfare policy, which is precisely what Don S. Kirschner found in an earlier study on social change in the early twentieth century, "The Ambiguous Legacy: Social Justice and Social Control in the Progressive Era," *Historical Reflections* 2 (June 1975), 69–88.

An extremely useful addition to the literature on the subject is a recent article by David A. Rochefort, "Progressive and Social Control Perspectives on Social Welfare," which appeared in *Social Service Review* 55 (Dec. 1981), 568–92. In this work, Rochefort first reviews the major themes and underlying assumptions that make up both the progressive and the social control models and the leading works on social welfare history and policy. He then identifies the major methodological problems they share in common, and ends with a discussion of the kinds of questions further theoretical work in this area must address — a fitting conclusion to this bibliographical note.

INDEX

Social Welfare or Social Control? has been set in ten point Times Roman with two points of spacing between the lines. Times Roman has also been used as display. The book was designed by Jim Billingsley, composed by Metricomp, Inc., printed offset by Thomson-Shore, Inc., and bound by John H. Dekker & Sons. The paper on which the book is printed bears the watermark of S. D. Warren and is designed for an effective life of at least three hundred years.

THE UNIVERSITY OF TENNESSEE PRESS ː KNOXVILLE